Come Walk with Me to Glory

What Being a Christian Means to Me

Dian Wells Matlock

iUniverse, Inc.
Bloomington

Come Walk with Me to Glory
What Being a Christian Means to Me

The views expressed in this work are solely those of the author and do not necessarily reflect the views of the publisher, and the publisher hereby disclaims any responsibility for them.

iUniverse books may be ordered through booksellers or by contacting:

iUniverse
1663 Liberty Drive
Bloomington, IN 47403
www.iuniverse.com
1-800-Authors (1-800-288-4677)

Because of the dynamic nature of the Internet, any web addresses or links contained in this book may have changed since publication and may no longer be valid.

Any people depicted in stock imagery provided by Thinkstock are models, and such images are being used for illustrative purposes only.

Certain stock imagery © Thinkstock.

ISBN: 978-1-4620-1201-5 (sc)
ISBN: 978-1-4620-1202-2 (hc)
ISBN: 978-1-4620-1204-6 (e)

Library of Congress Control Number: 2011906645

Printed in the United States of America

iUniverse rev. date: 1/6/2012

Table of Contents

Acknowledgments

Jesus spoke to Martha, the sister of Lazarus just before He raised Lazarus from the dead. Jesus said to her, "Did I not tell you and promise you that if you would believe and rely on Me, you should see the glory of God?" John 11:40 (Amp.)

The intensity of my soul's desire to seek God can be described somewhat through imagining the desperation of a deer that will die without a cool drink of water. Total exhaustion has caused his legs to barely be able to support him, and he has been running long and hard to escape a hunter. His run has brought him to the brink of death. He is exhausted, hot, and weary beyond further endurance. Nothing can or will be as wonderful as a cool drink from a mountain stream, which he wishes for with all his heart. Based on Psalm 42:1, we often hear the beautiful song that says, "As the deer panteth for the water, so my soul longeth after Thee. You alone are my heart's desire, and I long to worship Thee."

My soul does so earnestly seek the living God. He provided me with living waters to refresh my body, soul, and spirit. He rescued me, and I praise and thank Him with all my heart. Now the enemy runs from the powerful Word of God being spoken through me as a Christian. God has taught me the way of faith and about the weapon of the sword of the Lord, which is His Word. I am no longer just a sinner with a past. God has forgiven and forgotten what lies behind. I am now a Christian *with potential.*

He has taught me to stay close to Him; arm myself with His Word; have a joyful, praising spirit; and expect victory at every turn. He is real and stands behind His Word. I am zealous for the things of God because He has proven Himself to me through a lifetime of trials and sorrows. I don't resent Him because of the trials of life. No one escapes them, so face them His way and gain ground on Satan in spite of whatever harm he manages to do. I am grateful that God has taught me to face the enemy and then testify. The big picture here is that serious believers are the frontline soldiers of the army of the Lord. The focus is not on us or our trials; the focus is on victory for the Kingdom of God. I am so thankful for Him and am so glad that He loves me. If the trials of life refine us (according to our reaction to them) as pure gold, then I am well pleased to have the dross removed for my ultimate goal is Heaven, not things of this world. So, yes, I want to "drop the dross" and become a finer vessel with a testimony of His power displayed through a life of faith.

I would also like to thank my family for their love, patience, and support toward me during the writing of *Come Walk with Me to Glory*. Two years have now been spent from start to finish. I owe my son Greg and my daughter-in-law Brandy a thousand thanks for help with the computer and for previewing various sections with honesty and never-failing encouragement. They are precious in His sight and mine.

There is a group of folks at House of Mercy Church in Morris Chapel, Tennessee, that I would like to say a special thanks to, especially Pastor Dennis Moffett, his wife Diane, the inspiring singers of the choir she directs, and Ganetta Bishop, the precious Sunday school teacher of the ladies' class, along with those dear ladies. Together, they created the perfect environment of challenge and encouragement. I love everyone in that church with all my heart.

The person who would naturally sacrifice the most during a project like this would be one's spouse. This word of gratitude is written to honor my friend and my love, Rodg, my husband, who does truly have the patience of Job. His temperament and nature are a unique blend of quiet strength and patience. The independence he has allowed me in following this call on my life has been unwavering. He is very secure, encouraging, and kind. Thanks, Rodg. You are top-notch, numero uno, and man of the year in my book. Thanks for loving me, praying with me, standing with me, and being my good friend. There were times when your strength kept me able to go on, but it's not just those benefits that give me so much love for you—it's the man you are who won, and keeps, my heart. Thanks for being you. I will love you always.

Dian

Preface

(A True Short Story)

My friend Joyce Thompson, who is the administrator of a local nursing home, told me a story during a discussion we were having about how it is often unclear whether a person is saved or not. That is a very sad fact. People who love God usually let the love life flow. They want to be available to others in need, and their demeanor usually testifies to that through their smile, conversation, or behavior.

Joyce was reminded of how she had been concerned for her brother, who was severely mentally handicapped. He was unable to comprehend the message of salvation because he only had the mental capacity of a small child. She emphasized his lack of comprehension. His name was Clois Western, and at that time he was seventy-nine years old.

The day came when he was seriously ill and was not expected to live. Their mother had already gone on to glory. Joyce and her sister, Betty Hopper, had chosen to care for Clois at home for his last days so that he could feel the comfort of familiar faces. Joyce and Betty shared a bed in his room.

She said that late in the night, just before he died, she was awakened by the stunning sound of him singing that old hymn "I Saw the Light." She asked her sister whether she was awake or not, and Betty said that she was also hearing the miracle of that song. The sisters had no knowledge of him knowing the words to any song whatsoever and had never heard him sing before. Knowing that he had been touched by the loving hand of God, they felt gratefully assured regarding his eternal life.

The next day it became obvious that he had very little time left. He was restless and uneasy, and Joyce, who is also a nurse, believed that the end was near. Suddenly he became quiet, gazing toward the far upper corner of the room. Then he said in a clear and precise voice, "Tell her I can't fly." Joyce couldn't believe what she was hearing and asked, "What did you say?" He replied, saying again, "Tell her I can't fly." Realizing that an angel had come for him, she said, "Yes, you can." His last response was, "And Mama is there, too."

I have read about children having the same experiences as adults in near-death situations. Small children haven't been influenced or preprogrammed to tell of what they see in such experiences. Still, they have mentioned the bright light, beautiful colors, and similar things that people most often mention when they have encountered something outside and beyond consciousness, such as temporary death. Joyce's beautiful story about her mentally handicapped brother validates heavenly things existing beyond our human lives. What a lovely, true story, told by a loving sister who had tears welling up in her beautiful brown eyes.

Just to add a further note, though the story is really complete, one other thing happened that added to our amazement. The Sunday after she told me her story was a snowy day, and not many people made it to our church. My five-year-old granddaughter, Tylan Grace, had been very interested in the story when I had related it to our family. She asked me to teach her the song, "I Saw the Light," which I did. There was a casual, homey atmosphere in the sanctuary that day, with a smaller group than usual and everybody bundled up in wintery weather garb. I asked if Tylan Grace and I could give a short testimony. I told the congregation that the tiny "woman" with me was going to someday be anointed by God to speak out for Him, and I asked if they were okay with her singing one chorus of "I Saw the Light." She did so with enthusiasm and a big smile. (No fear here!) After that I told them Joyce's story, which was very touching to all hearts. A few days later I saw Joyce and told her what we had impulsively done, and that the testimony of her brother's wonderful parting was received with honor toward him. Again her eyes filled with tears. She said, "Dian, that was December the twenty-sixth—the anniversary date of his death. It was also on a Sunday, and it was snowing." God's grace is amazing, indeed.

There is an eternal life to be gained in Heaven. Jesus the Messiah is the Son of God. The Holy Spirit does dwell within us. How can people choose to not be familiar with our Creator in such a special and wonderful way? Great intensity regarding our mighty God should be born again in the heart of modern man. In today's world there's very little sense or reason in man's relationship (or lack of) with our holy God. Nothing even seems holy in this self-centered society. Yet there is so much wonder to be experienced and blessings to be received when we acknowledge the reality and glory of God.

I make no claim whatsoever to being a preacher, as everyone called by God is not forward. Once we have been born again we are all called to serve our individual purpose in His Kingdom, and my calling has been in interacting directly with people, becoming experienced in living and studying the Word and the principles of God, and being highly motivated toward living for God beyond the empty, powerless, and ineffective ways of "religious people." There are many who live by ritual, routine, and lack of a testimony that encourages the interest of nonbelievers. Living by genuine faith with life-changing results, victory, and joy is so much more effective as a testimony. It is my prayer that you will see God through the experiences and faith of my eyes. I have been eagerly willing to break free from religious ways and instead be a seeking, praising, believing Christian. In seeing Him through this very genuine and down-to-earth walk of faith, it is my prayer that you will be encouraged to discover the exciting and extraordinary life that is available to you too. It does require our sincere heart though, as appearances based on church attendance are not enough. I have put my life and the challenges of my life into God's hands. He never fails. They are now in your hands, too, so that you might benefit from what is to be learned through God's dealings with me. When I chose to respond appropriately to God's leading in the good times as well as the bad times, He has super-abundantly provided me with victory, good results, peace, and a happy heart, meeting my every need. God bless you in your considering a drastic, wonderful, life-changing life filled with love, confidence, peace, and joy from the very real, very alive, one and only true God.

God bless you.
Dian

A Snowy Day with a Friend

Looking out my window at the river and snow,
I pledged to spend my day with You,
Reading, praying, looking beyond
The beauty lying within my view.

It was pleasant, the scene around me—
The quiet and my sweet country life.
Snow falling and the fire so warming—
Then I felt Your presence and light.

I was reminded of Martha and Mary,
One busy, one wanting to hear,
And I knew Your glorious presence
Was instant for those drawing near.

Looking up to Heaven and closing my eyes,
I sought Your precious face.
In seeking an image, instead there shone through
Light—filling time and space.

It flooded my soul, gladdened my heart,
Gave me joy and surprise within.
I'm glad I spent my day with You,
And especially glad that You call me friend.

So what is it that shines so brightly
Through closed eyes in an upturned face?
Why, Lord, it is Your glory
When my soul seeks You out in praise.

My prayer is that you do come walk with
Me to glory.

Love forever,
Dian

Introduction

Concerning the Tree of Good and Evil

So God created man in His own image, in the image and likeness of God He created him; male and female He created them.
Genesis 1:27 (Amplified Bible)

Man was made in the image of our Creator. He made us chiefs in charge of the beautiful, peaceful providence that he had placed us in. He spoke the rest of our world into existence, but out of absolute love He formed us (Gen. 2:7) with His own hands. The act of forming implies that He took time and care.

He formed us on day six—the last day of His creation of the heavens and the earth. That made it perfectly clear that He had neither needed nor received any help from man—so no credit for man to take there. Then He formed man outside of paradise (Gen. 2:7–8, Amp), outside the Garden of Eden, from the dust of the ground, making us simple earthen vessels. We could make no claim to being made of gold, emerald, or diamond dust, or even soil from paradise—so, again, no credit for man to take over how we got here or what we're all made of. *All* credit goes to our awesome God for creating us; He is our Creator and our Father.

We should proclaim His power and love to the ends of the earth. We were His crowning glory, and we were meant to reflect His nature by the soul He breathed into us. We should praise His works and His majesty so that the world will have the knowledge that we do about what a magnificent God He is. The exceedingly amazing thing about it is that He is mindful of us and loves us. We are allowed the privilege of the care and friendship of the almighty, all-powerful, living God. Don't you find that truly amazing? Don't you want the rest of the world to know that our way of life as Christians is infinitely higher, richer, and miraculously greater than any other way of life? How can we be so passive about such an intensely wonderful opportunity? We should, without being prompted, be eager to tell of His goodness, mercy, power, and care. He gave us the earth, the animals, the mountains, the sea, and every possible thing we could need or be blessed by, and it is amazing to compare the way it was in the beginning to how it is now, near the end.

Man shuns God as though He doesn't exist, including a large number of "Christians" (except for their Sunday routine). Man goes about his earthly business with all his earthen vessel ability, not considering that he would have no business at all if it weren't for day six. We started out with honor and a free will, totally dependent on God, and now we are so very self-sufficient that we really think we have no time or need for Him at all. In spite of our great dishonor toward Him, He still offers us the honor of a one-on-one relationship with Him, and it is there for the asking. The offer of immortality for obedience and the threat of death for disobedience were first offered to the first man. Adam's soul was to rule his body, and God was to rule his soul. Man chose disobedience. That's how it all started, and that's how it still is, except for the size and the contemptuous audacity of it all.

Lust for everything opposed to God's way is never satisfied, but God and Heaven are still waiting for "whosoever will call on Him" to be saved (Acts 2:21, KJV). If hindsight is really twenty-twenty, then we have had plenty of time to see the error of our ways. Apparently we are blind in all directions without Him. In His hands there is wisdom, safety, promises, and love. Symbolically speaking, the Tree of Good and Evil is still set before us awaiting our choice—the blessing or the cursing, which will it be? If we continue in our perseverance against right choices and continue to purposefully make wrong choices, then we will not be able to live in eternity with Him in Heaven. When we choose to make choices according to His Word, then we can have eternal life in Heaven. We are constantly faced with opportunities to either obey God or to disobey Him. He gives us a free will to use and to choose. He does not force us; we make our own decisions, and blaming someone else doesn't work with Him. Adam blamed Eve and Eve blamed the snake, but they were both still directly accountable to God. From Joshua 24:15 (KJV) we hear, "Choose you this day whom you will serve, but as for me and my house, we will serve the Lord."

The world around us appears to have gone mad with selfishness, sin, dishonor, and taking freedoms not given by God. The world prefers to think that Christians are just out of touch—and many of us *are* out of touch with God, and sadly we seem to have no substantial message to offer.

Let's realign ourselves with Him and get busy. Our lives and our words should let the people in the world know that God is real and that He is a rewarder of those who seek Him. He provides for all our needs and gives us answers with power and love and kindness, always with our best interests in mind. Those worldly minded people surely would be so grateful for a way out if we did have enough credibility and courage to convince them of a far better way to live. If we would just show enough diligence in our faith to actually see the power of God displayed through answered prayer, we would have a good start.

There is so much loneliness, confusion, desperation, and despair. Don't you see that *we* hold the key? We have the knowledge but are not living by it or telling about it, and we have no right to disregard our holy God in such a way by ignoring Him and folks who are lost, those to whom He absolutely wants us to witness. Only we give ourselves the right to dishonor Him, especially when we live with the remarkable benefits and blessings that we have from Him and that we seem to expect from Him, often without even having given Him our heart.

The very same, very relevant God that provided the garden for Adam and Eve can and will provide anyone with their own personal garden if they sincerely ask. "Sincerely" is the key word. That's all they have to do—and our job is to simply and sincerely tell them. We who partake of the goodness of God through our acceptance of Christ's atoning blood owe it to Him and our fellowman. God's heart is longing for them to come in by accepting Jesus and His offer of salvation, and to have genuine goodness in their lives. God's heart is longing for us to obey and follow His orders in fulfilling the "Great Commission" that is given by Jesus as His last command to His disciples before He ascended into Heaven: "Jesus approached and breaking the silence said to them, All authority—all power of rule—in Heaven and on earth has been given to Me. Go then and make disciples of all the nations, baptizing them into the name of the Father and of the Son and of the Holy Spirit, teaching them to observe everything that I have commanded you, and lo, I am with you all the days, perpetually, uniformly and on every occasion—to the [very] close and consummation of the age. Amen—so let it be" (Matt. 28:18–20, Amp). Please note that He told the eleven disciples to make disciples (one who accepts and assists in spreading the doctrines of another) of all the nations. If one is a follower of Jesus and is saved by His blood, he is a disciple and is commissioned to go spread the Gospel also.

What if all the pebbles you don't drop in the pond make ripples that come back to you on Judgment Day? These are the pebbles that you didn't drop when you could have, such as the many opportunities we miss to offer prayer, help, or lifesaving hope when we are face-to-face with someone's specific need. Then what? Remember what you were really made of on the sixth day (the dust of the ground and the spirit of life from God), and how fragile you really are without God. Remember that the Spirit of God is holding it all together for you physically, emotionally, and spiritually—and that your real job is not to get too carried away with who you are, but to praise God, lead people to the Lord, and make it to Heaven yourself someday. The lure of the Tree of Good and Evil never stops beckoning, but if we keep God as the ruler of our soul, we can skip happily up to the pearly gate, and maybe He'll be able to say, "Well done, my good and faithful servant" (Matt. 25:21, KJV)—if in fact, we have done well.

We have a powerful testimony available to proclaim, one of amazing grace. We are *allowed* by God to have the kind of faith that can stop the rain for three and a half years, and then start it back again (Jas. 5:17). We have a God who makes all good things available to us, who heals the sick (Ps.103:2–3, Amp) and saves tormented souls. He brings joy, peace, and love. Do you really want to keep this wonderful news about our mighty God all to yourself, or do you want to share this good news and give glorious reviews to our Father and King?

Yes, He allows us the honor of being the instrument through which many of these blessings are bestowed on others, but remember how it happened on day six: all authority and power is from Him, and all praise goes to Him, so praise Him … and when you've done that, praise Him again.

May God bless you and keep you in His tender care. I love you all. Now, let's give glory to our Lord and our King. Amen, and again I say Amen.

Love,
Dian

Chapter One

Neither do I Condemn Thee

All praise, honor, and reverence goes to Father God; Jesus, my Savior; and our precious guide, the Holy Spirit—one mighty God, and so worthy to be praised.

God wrote the book of my life and gave me purpose. Our individual purpose can only be achieved when we each cooperate with our Creator. He wants to be our stronghold, our refuge, and our high tower. His love is great, and His truth will stand forever.

Confidence in who you are as His child, and who He is as your Father, brings peace beyond belief. God is real, has great power, is willing to use it in your behalf, and loves you. Fellow Christians love you too; you are not alone.

In beginning this book, I honestly did not know what particular subjects would be submitted for your consideration. After each chapter, there was no controlling human choice from me about the next topic; I chose to leave it up to God. In looking back over the subjects selected, I can see a list of priorities in which I was prompted and greatly assisted. There is honor and praise toward God. There is salvation, faith, forgiveness, God's will, unity, warnings, not being judgmental and not allowing man's doctrine to replace God's Word, taking up our spiritual weapons of warfare (Eph.6:12–20, Amp), believing the divinity and truth of the Bible, and then marching confidently as joyful Christians in the army of the Lord.

Sometimes the discipline within the army of the Lord gets confusing, especially when different leaders give contradicting orders. Sometimes people on the Lord's side start shooting others on the Lord's side, and then there is trouble in the camp. There are a few denominations that judge others as condemned for not following the doctrines of their particular denomination, and that has always been heavy on my heart. My concern is that in condemning others, these groups are aligned with those who, in their hearts, commit spiritual murder. They choose to disqualify people and consider other denominations as *unsaved*, even though those people firmly believe in Jesus and have accepted Him as their Lord and Savior according to John 3:3, John 3:16, and Romans 10:9–10. If, through human error and judgment, you are pitching a fellow believer into hell—which would be his or her destination if he or she isn't saved—is that not assigning him or her to the spiritual death of his or her soul? According to the condemning spirit, it is equal to a death sentence for him or her. I believe that we are allowed to know and to judge right from wrong behavior according to God's Word, but we cannot judge someone's soul.

> **If we could all meet at the Cross of Jesus and work together, forgetting the doctrinal details, then we could be a much stronger, brighter, more successful church that would war against the enemies of Christ—and not each other.**

Even though we can believe that other Christian denominations have had erroneous, different, or less teaching, we shouldn't smugly belittle them to the point of them being infidels in our minds. That's not Christ-like, folks.

Jesus said in Matthew 5:21–22, "You have heard it was said of old, 'You shall not murder, and whoever murders will be in danger of the judgment.' But I say to you that whoever is angry with his brother without a cause shall be in danger of the judgment." *The Spirit Filled Life Bible,* under the heading of "Murder Begins in the Heart," makes this statement: "The sixth Commandment not only prohibits the actual deed of murder, but extends to thought and word, to unrighteous anger and destructive insults." *The Matthew Henry Study Bible* explains that the Jewish teachers of the law were content with punishment against the external and "laid no restraint upon the inward lusts, from which wars and fightings come." The error was that they prohibited only the sinful act, not the sinful thought. The commandment from God addresses both in the same way and is worth thinking about.

It is very hurtful to feel alienated from a group of people that you love dearly and who have treated you with love and respect—until they found out that you were water baptized in a way different from their belief! Suddenly, *you* were an infidel in their eyes. If your heart is full of love for them—and if you refuse to argue the point or to compromise your own belief, knowing that the spirit of deception remains as a wall between you—you have no choice but to leave, with great sadness and loss. When it happened to me, there were two main reasons why I could not simply stay. The first was that their devotion to their belief kept me targeted as one needing conversion.

Many years ago, my worldly unsaved *spirit* had been baptized into the most sacred *Spirit* of Jesus by truly and deeply believing in Him as the Son of God. I had repented for my sins and had received Him through this spiritual baptism—not intellectually or physically. Acts 2:38 refers to a spiritual baptism into the belief of all that Jesus is, and it follows repentance. Declare and do away with past sins in honesty before God. It cleans you up for the new life that you are about to be given when you receive the nature of Jesus. Those whose spirits are baptized into His spirit are born again from above and have a new spiritual nature. Being born again by spiritual means can only occur through God and *spiritual means*, not through any physical acts that man can perform. The Holy Spirit becomes operative in every believer during this supernatural, spiritual change. Following that, I was then baptized in water according to Matthew 28:19. After the spiritual change, one is constantly hoping from then on to display more and more of His nature and character and to be like Him. That is true baptism according to the original language of the Bible. I had later received a fuller measure by being filled with the Holy Spirit (Acts 1:8; 19:2-6). That occurs when desired and received by faith.

The second reason that I could not stay was because I consider it my duty and my desire to invite others to church. I could not be responsible for our guests becoming indoctrinated into beliefs that the Bible does not teach regarding the basic steps of salvation. Believe spiritually, receive spiritually, then be water baptized physically to identify with Jesus in death and rising again to a newness of life. On two different occasions I have lost church families because of that same reason. It is wrong for churches to label themselves as nondenominational to appeal to many, when some are really practicing a very specific, man-made denomination with doctrinal issues that conflict with the grace and Word of God. However, I am still blessed by the joy that I shared with them in the beginning before I understood their underlying beliefs. I love them with all my heart and still believe through faith that God's influence will redirect their attention toward the Holy Trinity (or Tri-unity) of God. Having my belief in the Trinity (which is discussed later in chapter eight) spiritually challenged every time I attended, seemed to be causing many of them to sin by their denial of the Trinity, for which I didn't want to be responsible. I longed for a church family that I was accepted as a part of, with love and support being our objective toward each other, and with all of us standing shoulder to shoulder in strong, unified agreement regarding our mission for the lost. Being Christians in true nondenominational churches can give one more openness for compatibility with others, praise, joy, and freedom to love and be loved without reservation.

This is just one example of our focus not being kept on the sacrifice of Jesus on the cross and the crown of thorns that Jesus endured for us. Pray that God's chosen people will accept the truth of His blood being shed to cover the sins of man. I would do anything for Him. People can let us down, but Jesus never will. Experience has taught me to keep my eye on the prize.

These are some areas in which we should improve, and our commitment to God should become fuller, richer, deeper and more profound. Pettiness and littleness of spirit should be rebuked; pride and dignity should be cast down. The effect of knowing the living God personally should sing out in our spirit, with the presence of Jesus and the Holy Spirit so manifested in our souls that we practically glow. One of the meanings of "manifest" is to "cause to shine." We live in a worldly environment that is hostile to God and to Christians because our ethics, standards, morals, and beliefs are different from the world's. However, they need us. Is the manifest presence of Jesus causing you to shine and to be identifiable among all peoples, or has a spirit of another kind made you want to blend in and not be noticed, or to not be challenged about it? Where's the stand we're supposed to take for the Gospel's sake, so that we are serving our purpose toward the lost? At the same time that we are following God's plan for mankind, a great benefit emerges. We are the blessed ones, and we begin to realize that the problems we have allowed to rule our thoughts and minds just aren't what it's all about. We have biblical ways to defeat the negatives that come against us in life. We shouldn't be intimidated by the world's ways, even though our enemy (Satan) is aggressive. There are a lot more unsaved people in the world than saved, and their ways are to try to influence our thinking to fit in with theirs! After all, it is all they know, and they want us to conform. However, we walk about on this earth as spirits living in our human form that will be glorified in Heaven someday. While we're here, we happily rely on the fact that we are really citizens of Heaven (Heb. 3:20, Amp) and are only temporarily residing here on earth. We've been given a mission, and it isn't to fit in or to be lukewarm. Revelation 3:16 (KJV) states, "So then because thou art lukewarm, and neither cold nor hot, I will spue thee out of my mouth." We are to take a stand for Jesus in a loving way, but as militant soldiers against evil, using the full armor of God, doing our job, not being cowards, and most definitely not being ashamed of the Gospel.

This world is a testing ground. It can be difficult or very appealing and distracting to our flesh in thousands of ways. It is the devil's job to trick or deceive us any way he can; don't be tricked or fooled by his worldly attractions. We all have been at times, but we need to focus on avoiding those traps. They produce nothing of real value or substance except for points won for the devil's team. Resist them. Recognize that worldly interests (the worldly environment apart from God) are empty wastes of the time God has given us, of our energy, and of our resources. Evaluate your lifestyle; live for God and seek a high standard of wholesome living for yourself and your family. What a different world it could be if that became our focus and our priority. God has always advised us well, and man has always reaped great rewards when following His advice. On the other hand, remember the one bite from that appealing apple, and the devastation that occurred?

Take up your cross—it is not irksome or burdensome (1 John 5:3, Amp), as the world wants you to think. It's a small load to carry for such a grand and magnificent prize. Love the people who persecute you and be a good example. Pray earnestly for them and help them see the truth and the good life in Godly living. Don't be influenced by the constant pull and the sights and sounds of ungodly, worldly ways. The frenzy of the world's decline is becoming greater and more out of control every day. Stop and think about what you are doing with your time and attention while distress and disaster hammer at the door. Why are people acting like ostriches with their heads in the ground? It would be nice if the theory of trying not to notice would just make it all go away, but that's not reality. Time is short and the end is near.

For nearly thirty years now, my heart has longed for God with a steadfast yearning to actively serve Him and to pursue deeper, richer insight into His ways, into who He really is and into what He really wants from us.

**New Life Books – Dian, Ralph, and
the legendary Larnell Harris**

In being either co-owner or owner of three wonderful Christian bookstores, I have enjoyed the opportunity of having access to numerous enlightening Christian books, and to also serve the American public in both public and private ministry. An open door was there for both the Christian and non-Christian world to have access to me, and for me to respectfully have access to them. Our stores were nondenominational, and my perspective is from that rare point of view. We loved all our customers without condition, by our spirit, and without placing religious boundaries on them. Biblical guidelines are not the same as man's discriminating rules.

> **The emphasis of this book is on the truth, magnificence, and holiness of God. Examine your personal responsibility for your own salvation, and know how to question the method with which you were led to believe that you had escaped hell forever. If you have uncertainty about whether or not you are saved, becoming saved is biblically stated in simple terms. Perhaps you are saved but feel in your heart that there is something more that you need to know about God, and there is.**

We never learn it all while on this earth, but the more we know, the happier we are and the better we behave. It doesn't become a list of "nos and don'ts," but rather a list of "yeses and dos." The world views Christianity in a negative way. The truth is Christianity is a very positive, exciting, joyful way to live. How can the world trump seeing miracles, having prayers answered, and actually having a personal relationship with the living God? Everything they achieve is surrounded by darkness, produced through lust, fear, and greed. Everything God's children achieve is surrounded by light, produced by His favor, promises, and love.

Let me give you one exciting example. Have you ever heard anyone mention the Shekinah (glory), where in Isaiah's vision (Is. 6:1–4) the divine presence of God filled the temple? Did you know that if your church sought the manifestation of the almighty God's divine presence, He could really make Himself known to the people? I do not know, nor does any human, what precise conditions must exist in order for that to happen, but the point is, is anybody talking about, or seeking such a magnificent event for the sake of the church and the people? In chapter 11 there will be an example of God revealing His presence.

God is in the New Testament as well as the Old, and He is not restricted from being anywhere, anytime, or any place that He pleases. God said, "Let Us [Father, Son, and Holy Spirit] make mankind in our image" (Gen. 1:26, Amp). Therefore, the Holy

Spirit and Jesus are also evident in the Bible from beginning to end. God's Word is called the Living Word. God breathed life from Himself into us when we were formed. When we continue to breathe in the Living Word, which is alive and which goes forth to accomplish its purpose (Is. 55:11, Amp), then we are living vitally united to our Creator and can continue on in our destiny toward eternal life with Him. Isaiah 61:11 (Amp) describes the Word as having "self-fulfilling power." When it is put or kept on or in something, it accomplishes what it is sent forth to do. We need to realize that the Bible is not just a book. John 1:1 (Amp) says, "In the beginning [before all time] was the Word [Christ], and the Word was with God, and the Word was God Himself."

We need to be aware that it is our personal responsibility to stay vitally united. In John 15:1–7 (Amp), we find that God is the Vinedresser, Jesus is the True Vine, and we are the branches. Please note that "branches" begins with a lowercase "b." God's titles are capitalized—not ours. It says that we are cleansed and pruned because of the Word, and that we should abide in Him. If we do not dwell in Him, we are thrown out as a broken-off branch and wither. Such branches are gathered up and thrown into the fire and they are burned.

Think of the Bible as the *Living* Word of God. That will keep you more in the reality of Him.

> **Walking with God is the pinnacle of all that is good and worth striving for on earth, and it is a blessed and lovely way to live. Choose to allow trust in Him to bring order to any chaos or need that may be in your life. It is a decision that you personally make in your heart, and it will not be based on any religious ritual. You will never regret it. My suggestion is to encompass extreme (by the world's standards) Christianity. Being mediocre in anything is to withhold excellence. Seeking the excellence of God is an exciting quest.**

I have sometimes pleased God, but I have also failed Him. There have been times when I was a coward and other times when I braved live TV or actual physical danger when concerned with the needs of others. In our good behavior or bad, God will always be constant, true, and keep our best interests in mind. In holding everything up to the light of His glory, an overall view caused some shockingly obvious areas to rise to the top with warning flags waving. Years of observation, study, and experience have produced the evidence presented here. Problem areas result from the subtle deception of that same sly serpent that lurked in the Tree of Good and Evil: Satan, enemy of God and man.

The dangers have become great threats to Christianity because they are being ignored and are growing. They lie in our complacency and in the fact that we have stopped challenging evil. Other areas would be in whether or not our prayer lives are effective, or whether or not we really have confidence in God. You may challenge yourself about what being a Christian *really* means to you. That question, asked of yourself, sounds simple, but it is legitimately profound. Evaluate your personal testimony and recognize, for example, the paralyzing effect of not forgiving others, or yourself.

The power of faith is a must-have for Christians. Faith is not a wimpy, illusive expression of hope; it is the result and product of hope. It is a powerful, active, spiritual law, but you must use it to see its extraordinary benefits. My life is living proof of that spiritual principal of God making a way when there seemed to be none. My personal testimony is woven throughout, and chapter 10 reveals one way that God provided a specific communication to me. It is very cool to know that the thoughts in your head and heart can be direct communication from the living God.

This book exemplifies to some degree the intensity that should be born in the heart of modern man. There's very little sense or reason surrounding modern man in his relationship with our holy God. Nothing even seems holy in today's self-centered society. Judgment Day may bring wailing and gnashing of teeth, but of course that will be far too late.

> **We shouldn't be deprived of God's majestic power and glory by what another person says or fails to mention. Read for yourself about the miracles, love, protection, and goodwill that God has in store for those who do seek and long for Him. Don't believe it when a person tells you that spiritual gifts within the body of Christ no longer exist, because they definitely do. I can tell you with great enthusiasm that the only limits put on God are put there by man. Chapter 11 proclaims the wonder and power of God's presence by still showing up when sought by His children. He has been neither boring nor lacking in benevolence.**

Man has practically suffocated the life out of Jesus's body, the Church, with an overload of doctrine, rules, humdrum, and "in decency and in order" as referred to in 1 Corinthians 14:40 (KJV). Whoever said that there couldn't be decency and order in robust praise and prayer? Folks aren't being indecent and disorderly when they praise God enthusiastically. The Bible actually tells us to seek the gifts of the spirit; read it to see for yourself, please. Gifts of the spirit and prayer are the real keys to knowing God. Don't be afraid of God; run to Him, not from Him. There is so much to be gained by believing that nothing is too big or too difficult for Him. Love Him and trust Him, and when you do, watch the amazing results as they unfold. Look and hope for Him. That's where amazing grace comes in. Any and all who choose to can walk in an amazing relationship with the living God.

My focus is to elevate God and to verify that there are great benefits, protection, and peace that come from trusting Him. Even with increased interest, we are only scratching the surface. Show Him honor and find out whether or not your eternity with Him is secured. One should seek to be truly saved. Whatever your place may be—whether a baby Christian still on the milk of the

Word, or a more mature Christian on the meat of the Word (Heb. 5:12–14)—He loves you. It can truly be said, though, that there is an extraordinary personal walk with Him available to those who actively and sincerely seek Him.

Being saved means that you have recognized that having Jesus as your Savior is the only way to Heaven. Shame on people who disrespect our holy God by saying that there are other ways in which one can receive salvation. In 1 Corinthians 15:1–4 (Amp), Paul says that the Gospel—the glad tidings of salvation—had been proclaimed, welcomed, and accepted. Faith came by which people were saved—if they held fast and kept firmly to what was preached, and if they did not believe at first *without effect*. He explained that Christ, the Messiah and the anointed one, died for our sins in accordance with what the scriptures foretold in Isaiah 53:5–12. To become saved, one must hear the Gospel and then receive it as a truth so that it is internalized. It must be so real to you that you consider it the foundation on which you will build the rest of your life, and that you are willing to take a stand for it.

Becoming saved includes repentance, which means that you agree to turn and go in the opposite direction from sin, and that you are sorry for the sins that you have committed already. Jesus does not expect perfection from any human being, but He wants us to have a willing heart. You agree to accept His righteousness that He imparts to you when His spirit lives within your heart and soul. Your heart should be truly changed, with you having a brand-new attitude. You must understand that you are accepting His sacrificial death on the cross as having been done for you personally, and that you sincerely recognize and receive the offer of His blood having covered your sins and freed you from the bondage of sin and spiritual death. You truly believe that Jesus is the Son of God and that He died and rose from the dead. You also should understand that He is now in Heaven, at the right hand of God, but He is coming back for His church. That return for us is referred to as the Rapture, which is an English word used to describe "gathering in" or "catching away". The Wuest

New Testament, an Expanded Translation, says it best within 1 Thessalonians: 4:17. It says "we shall be snatched away forcibly in [masses of saints having the appearance of] clouds for a welcome-meeting with the Lord in the lower atmosphere." That event may be approaching soon. Becoming saved is a simple, humble approach to a relationship that can go as far as you choose, according to your faith. When your acceptance is serious, then you will have entered into a relationship with the God who rides on the wings of glory. It should be a profound experience because your sins have been forgiven and your soul has been saved from eternal fire.

My tears are shed over the hope for all lost people to become saved. If we truly love and honor God, we will willingly seek out and help lead others to eternal life with Him. When His mission becomes our mission, we will be living witnesses to the way, the truth, and the life. Be unstoppable!

A new life was created within me by the supernatural Holy Spirit of our glorious and supernatural God. He and all good things of God are readily available to all who believe, so come— walk with me to glory.

I have signed each chapter with either love or a blessing, as God has placed in my heart to do. He is the divine connection between you and me, and if I met you, God within my heart and soul would cause me to love you, because He does. He is our Father; He is our Friend. If I seem to praise Him often, just think of it as a song of praise that is in my heart and is ever with me. He is the glorious power, and we have the privilege to adore Him. He is enthroned in our praises (Ps. 22:3), so seek His presence and let Him be praised. Participate in the joy with me as He dwells in the praises of His people. Amen.

Love in Christ Jesus,
Dian

Chapter Two

North or South

We need to decide for ourselves, after we reach an age of accountability, whether we want to spend eternity in the cool, upper, lofty northern atmosphere, or whether we prefer an extremely hot, lower, southern atmosphere in the confines of the earth. Not only is it nice to be able to know where you will spend eternity, but you also get to make your own choice; no one else can possibly make it. It is incorrect, according to God's Word, for you to assume that you are safe based on opinions or rituals, even if they did occur with great ceremony, seriousness, beauty, and holy attire. You must know what you are doing and do it by choice, motivated by desire and commitment. No man knows, and no human is holy enough to declare, whether another person will go to Heaven or not. Neither can a man declare you worthy or not. No person can go to Heaven simply because he belongs to an exclusive group that claims to have the right to provide their members with an automatic "right of entry." Each is on his own, so whether or not you go is up to your sincerity and consequent actions. After that, it's in God's hands. It doesn't matter if you are a star-studded Christian or if you look like a bedraggled bird that a cat has harassed. Neither your title, education, bank account, nor holy attire will qualify you, and neither will your poverty nor your suffering. We each have to work out our own personal relationship—one-on-one with Him. Only He is holy. Only He paid the sacrificial price. Only He can determine each person's entry—or exclusion—into the wonderful and so greatly prized eternal life beyond the grave with Him. Both eternities will be forevermore.

The only holiness that people possess is Christ living within their heart and the precious Holy Spirit of the living God within their souls. That is the way to Heaven, and that blessing from God makes us want to be more holy in our attitude and behavior. Holiness is described in the *Amplified Bible* as "separation from sin, with simple trust and hearty obedience" (Ps. 93:5).

Since the beginning of mankind, people have wanted to control others, even to the extent of deciding the fate of another's soul. No one can, so don't be fooled and don't be worried. The truth is this: we are each responsible as individuals for being in the constant process of recognizing, accepting, obeying, respecting, and honoring our loving, magnificent Lord. Jesus died so that we could live, and He wants us in Heaven with Him when our human life is over.

It is so simple. He is God of all. We are barely more than little clay dolls. He breathed life into us, gave us intelligence and spirit and freewill choice. He is also giving us the opportunity to be counted among the blessed folks whose God-motivated choices have obtained them the right to coexist with God in Heaven someday.

If He had been the only influence to choose from, then there wouldn't have had to be a choice. Don't you think that choices were given to see which we would make, and who would turn out to be His true children? The Tree of Good and Evil was put before Adam and Eve, and look what devastation occurred. They're our ancestors, you know. We are forewarned through their example against the "Adam and Eve spirit," which would be one of disobedience. We don't seem to have purged it out of the human race as time has moved along, but we are definitely given the opportunity to take a stand against it. Parents should be aware of the effect of how that spirit will affect their children's character and lives, and what a responsibility they have to be the right kind of examples to their children. This worldly environment in which we live, and which is controlled by Satan, is our other choice. When Christians refer to the world (as opposed to Christianity), we are describing the system of operation that is not ruled by God. Communism, socialism, and terrorism are examples of Satan's destroying, deceptive power over the human spirit. Those evils are from Satan, but they are nothing as compared to him. He equals misery. He equals lies. He equals hell.

So there we have it. First and always there is God, representing all good things, and most of all divine love. Then we have mankind in between. Next, the serpent Satan represents enticement, greed, pride, lust, and all of the "soul-stealers." These are what we have to choose between. Good and bad; light and dark; love and hate. It seems simple, doesn't it? Yet millions refuse the good life that God offers and instead think they are better off and having fun by choosing Satan. They become slaves to his ideas and allow him to dictate to them, control them, and eventually ruin their lives. When we love and honor God, we are able to see Satan as he is, from the perspective of our being outside his domain. Inside his domain may look appealing to some, with drugs, sex, vanity, pornography, lies, deceit, and evil—convincing people that they should have and do whatever they like or want. Calling him the deceiver fits him well. *No one* who follows Satan's ways of life will win. Those people are, by their own personal choice, choosing hell. God cannot be blamed; He made His way very available. See what influence Satan gained over mankind in man's fall in the Garden of Eden (Gen. 3:6–8, Amp). His slithering trick occurred under very nonthreatening conditions, while man (and woman) stood innocently beside a beautiful tree, the Tree of Good and Evil. We are standing by it too with every decision we make, though it can't physically be seen.

When the Lord God formed man out of the dust, we became living beings. He had hoped to see seeds of spiritual fruit, righteousness, and good things sown in the soil that we were

16

made of. His Word sows seeds of harvest into our lives that were meant to multiply and spread the good news all over the land. Sadly, those good things, like love, charity, and hope, which are meant to grow and bless others, are often never watered or nourished, so they wither. Instead, many choose to feed their spirit with buckets of Satan's evil ways, such as selfishness, greed, complacency toward God, and more. Doesn't that sound like a diet folks would refuse if they were thinking about what they were doing to themselves, their children, and their own future, especially after the dust has returned to dust? Old slew-foot really is out there trying to get anybody he can—but remember this quote, which I saw on a church billboard: "With God there is an endless hope. Without Him there is a hopeless end." Choose to believe God and that He gave us Jesus, who died for our sins and who loves and wants us in His family.

To witness the transition of a slow, unattractive, vulnerable caterpillar into a beautiful, harmless butterfly, with escape built into its delicate wings, is to see the parallel of a sinner becoming a born-again child of God. The butterfly is able to soar upward and to avoid danger. We are able to approach our Father in Heaven and to find safety in Him. Just as the butterfly is harmless and delicate, we too must do no harm. The butterfly has physical wings; we have God's Word of promises and power. As the butterfly must protect its wings, we too must guard our escape mechanism (His Word hidden in our heart). All of God's creatures and people have natural enemies, so staying aware of whatever harm might be around us is necessary. Many lovely butterflies have had beautiful summer days end by being pinned inside a collector's display case. You can see how the parallel continues. Our own choices decide whether we soar upward or plummet downward.

Have you ever seen a predator play with its prey, like a cat with a wounded bird? The poor bird doesn't have a chance, even though at some point before the catastrophe, the bird did have capable wings. Obviously it didn't use them in time, but it could have. We can assume that "disregard" caused it to "not regard" the warning signs or the danger. I suppose that it was in its own little world and didn't take flight while it could—but safety *was* available, because cats can't fly.

When Jesus comes into your heart, His holiness dwells within you and provides you with the right to His righteousness, which in turn provides you with the right to be in right-standing with God. That is something only God can do, and even though you may love your spiritual mentor or pastor, your love for God should be far greater. His holiness within us not only gives us credibility as Christians, but it is also what gets us into Heaven. It is only God's holiness within us—not ours or anyone else's. He offers so much more than anything we can ever hope for or imagine. He did actually die a very painful and humiliating death for us. Don't think that because He is God, He made the pain disappear. He suffered it on purpose, for us—to take it for us, in our place. Can't we be sensitive and kind enough in return to truly love Him back? That's not asking very much from us for having received such a gift.

If the ticket (free pass) you hold in your hand says, "Going north" ("Going up"), it should be evidenced by love. If we really want to be in God's army, then we need to examine our hearts and be willing to step it up. All would agree that Christians are in active, vigorous conflict against evil, which results in spiritual warfare. As warring participants for good, we are members of God's mighty army. In Hebrews 2:10 (KJV), Christ is referred to as the captain of salvation. Paul refers to his brother and companion in labor as a soldier (Phil. 2:25, KJV). Ephesians 6:10–18 directs us to put on the full armor of God, and it is metaphorically based on the battle dress of a Roman soldier of the first century.

> **We are to take up our position, be aggressive, establish strongholds, and still be standing after a confrontation, ready for the next battle. This is not armor simply for passive protection, but it is for offensive warfare—and victory.**

(Now would be a good time for an enthusiastic war cry!) With the sword of the Lord and the shield of faith, we are destined to win. How can anyone dislike the assurance of knowing they're on the winning side? When we do arrive at the finish line, you will not find me back in camp but joyfully in the heat of battle. "What then shall we say to [all] this? If God be for us, who [can be] against us?—Who can be our foe, if God is on our side?" (Rom. 8:31, Amp). Amen, Lord. So let it be. Do we love the Gospel enough to fight for it?

Christians will say that they love God, but here is a question to ask yourself about how much you really love Him. When I first read this scripture in the Wuest New Testament, it surprised me because of how different it was asked compared to the King James Version. Because the Wuest New Testament is a literal translation, the sentence structure is different, but it is easy to understand. Jesus was questioning Peter about the level of Peter's love for Jesus, and this is the same question we all need to contemplate. In John 21:15, the Wuest New Testament says, "Then when they had breakfasted, Jesus says to Simon Peter, 'Simon, son of Jonas, do you have a love for me called out of your heart by my preciousness to you, a devotional love that impels you to sacrifice yourself for me?'" The honest answer Peter first gave was, "Yes Lord, as for you, you know positively that I have an emotional fondness for you." The second time he was asked, Peter said that he had "a friendly feeling" toward Jesus. The third time he was asked, Peter was grieved. How do we measure up to a question as sensitive and real as that? There are different degrees of love. Jesus's question refers to agape love, or the God kind. Peter's answer was a less emphatic kind of love that didn't show complete devotion. After Peter received the Holy Spirit, he used the agape form of the word in his writings about Jesus, much to his credit.

The Lord replied by telling Peter to feed His lambs (sheep). That is also the great commission for us to follow, as a way of showing our love toward God and our fellowman. If we have servants' hearts and show enough love to other people by sharing the Gospel with them, it also tells God through our actions and obedience that we really do love Him, that we are willing to share the Gospel and all the wonderful benefits available through the love and provision of our kind God. That is putting the right kind of works with our faith. It is also love beyond emotional fondness, or having a friendly feeling. Jesus's eyes were ever searching for whomever He could help. I want my eyes to be ever searching too, instead of being so easily distracted—or worse, centered on myself.

There is another tough test on how (not whether) we really love God. Would you be able to give up all fear? This does not mean that one should test God by throwing caution to the wind by doing such things as swallowing poison, feeding a wild bear, or jumping out of a plane without a parachute! We are not to "test" God with unnatural foolishness. But believe it or not, true, deep, mature love for God trusts Him so much that it can say, "No matter what, I am not afraid. I trust you, Father God, with everything." First John 4:18 (Amp) really inspires us to reach for more because it challenges us to give fear up—and that means all fear, such as of death, illness, the night, speaking in public, failure, and anything else you can think of that is against God's Word. His Word is truth; we need to believe it. This question about fear will be a gauge to measure your love for God within yourself. It is testing my love too, but I am determined to press on against that force of fear being generated from the wrong source. We search out things that are sugar free or fat free. Wouldn't it be grand if we sought and achieved a fear-free life? The referenced scripture reads as follows: "There is no fear in love—dread does not exist, but full-grown (complete, perfect) love turns fear out of doors and expels every trace of terror! For fear brings with it the thought of punishment, and (so) he who is afraid has not reached the full maturity of love—is not yet grown into love's complete perfection."

After the shock of that last statement, the question had to be asked: "Are there really people who love God that much and who can faith the fear away?" After a brief moment of thought, the challenge arose in my heart, and much progress has been made since that day. I will also add that defeating the spirit of fear through trust and practice has been a great advantage to me in many situations. Life with God is fun because He never lets you down! If we believe that something is a sure thing, like God's Word, it's not really stretching our faith to believe it, is it? Sometimes things appear at first glance to be harder than they really are. Most of us are probably programmed to react in fear. Because faith-building exercises benefit us in our journey through our natural lives, practicing on a sure thing is a good way to develop good new habits. After a while you start operating on automatic pilot, and life gets even sweeter. Trust is so much more comfortable than fear. Allowing ourselves to worry about things is one of the greatest challenges that we face. Worry, anxiety, and stress mean we are not turning things completely over to God, and we are deciding that we need to figure out how to take care of them ourselves. Seeking wisdom and giving thought to trials of life is not the same as worry. In looking at the idea from the outside, worrying looks like a foolish thing for us to do, but how often we do go there. Worry is based in f-e-a-r. Try "worrying" in the positive by thinking, "What if (the bad thing you're thinking about) *does not* happen? What if it actually happens the way it should?" Think of faith versus fear as a coin that you might flip. If heads is faith and tails is fear, then get a coin with heads on both sides! The only way to have peace in the midst of a storm is to trust God and turn our lives over to Him.

Fear does sometimes come against me, to the point of making me physically sick. The last time it happened, I had been asked to share something from this book with a church group. During the last few minutes before the pastor called me up, when it was far too late to escape by flight, fear clutched me like paralysis. I was terrified and was convinced that when they asked me to go to the podium, I would simply faint. But God rescued me. At the last minute He told me to reveal that evil spirit of fear to the congregation. That gave me enough hope to make it to the center of the platform. As soon as I started to speak, I said that I knew there was no need for me to be afraid of my brothers and sisters in Christ, but that Satan had put a spirit of fear on me that was terrible and overwhelming. "So be subject to God. Stand firm against the devil; resist him and he will flee from you" (Jas. 4:7, Amp). I asked that they all pray with faith and help me rebuke the spirit, for I was determined to fulfill what God had sent me to do. They all started praying and resisting him by the Word of God. Then, where Satan had been showing his ugliness, the Holy Spirit, who had been there all along, was revealed, and He most certainly did prevail. He blessed us mightily for our trust in how to overcome through His powerful Word. Faith and the courage to believe led me on.

God knew what was going to happen in that church and that I would hold my position against the enemy. I wasn't provided with that information in advance because I needed to endure the trial and learn that I could face down the enemy. He also knew that I would learn from it and that it would offer a lesson in trust and determination to others at the same time. It could easily have ruined the rest of the night and been an unforgettable evening by me landing on the floor with a very faithless testimony, instead of what we overcame to enjoy, which became unforgettable in a great way later. It was a trial, and He knew about the good that would come from it. It was a night that I shall never forget; it was one of the worst attacks of fear that I have ever been subjected to. Human self-interest was all on the line—pride, dignity, ability to speak, or possibly even to stand upright—it was all placed before God and in His hands. With the congregation knowing the obvious sheer terror and public humiliation that was upon me, followed by seeing an act of determined obedience, a living testimony unfolded before my eyes and theirs—especially the eyes of the youth, who I suspect were anticipating a somewhat boring evening. How absolutely grand the entire event turned out to be, with Satan revealed and then defeated, with God revealed and, as always, victorious. This was not about me. I was hardly more than an instrument—except for having a will with which to choose and a determination to not be stopped before getting to where God had told me to go. That may have been one of those times when I risked my life by pressing on. A heart attack didn't seem farfetched to me at the moment! "Let God arise, let His enemies be scattered" (Ps.68:1, KJV). Chapter 11 continues with the glorious outcome of this challenging event.

If anyone questions whether or not fear is a spirit, then please read 2 Timothy 1:7–9 (Amp), which states, "For God did not give us a spirit of timidity—of cowardice, of craven and cringing and fawning fear—but [He has given us a spirit] of power and of love and of calm and well-balanced mind and discipline and self-control. Do not blush or be ashamed then to testify to and for our Lord, nor of me, a prisoner for His sake, but [with me] take your share of the suffering [to which the preaching] of the Gospel [may expose you, and do it] in the power of God. [For it is He] Who delivered and saved us and called us with a calling in itself holy and leading to holiness—that is, to a life of consecration, a vocation of holiness; [He did it] not because of anything of merit that we have done, but because of and to further His own purpose and grace (unmerited favor) which was given us in Christ Jesus before the world began—eternal ages ago."

When we love God as we should, we don't find His ways to be burdensome or irksome. "For the [true] love of God is this, that we do His commands—keep His ordinances and are mindful of His precepts and teaching. And these orders of His are not irksome—burdensome, oppressive or grievous. For whatever is born of God is victorious over the world; and this is the victory that conquers the world, even our faith" (1 John 5:3–4, Amp). We just listen for the instruction and then do it. Usually man likes to add his own opinion, though, complicating things.

One thing most often complicated is the manner in which we show love toward our fellow man. Usually, it is by holding him up to the light to see if there are any flaws in him. That's not godly, folks. Jesus asks us how it is that we look for a speck in our brother's eye when we have a board in our own (Matt. 7:3, Amp). Let me say it this way: we all have flaws, and criticism of others doesn't make our flaws disappear. From the way I understand it, our attempts to diminish others is an attempt to elevate ourselves— which means that we have fear, because that's really what it is. If we can reduce someone to allegedly be beneath us, then that seems to elevate us above them in our estimation, which we then try to convince others of also. It's self-consciousness, lack of self-worth, or fear that they will be liked or accepted or favored above us. We need to recognize the spirit of fear (2 Tim. 1:7), rebuke it, and be happy to have the gifts and unique qualities that we each do; then, we should help those folks we've trampled to get up off the floor because they're God's children, too.

Others' ways may vary from ours. This is not referring to sinful ways but rather to customs, rituals, or things that do not actually affect their salvation. Jesus never told us to hold our denomination up as the way to salvation. His path is straight and narrow (Matt. 7:13–14, Amp), as revealed clearly in His Word, and everybody who professes to love God should respond to His direct, uncomplicated instructions. We can share the Gospel, help and encourage one another, pray and discuss how to keep to the narrow path, and communicate lovingly among other denominations without controversy. Man's judgments, habits, and rituals were not part of the Gospel. The army of the Lord has people of all sorts and sizes, and from different walks of life. There are various lengths of time in service, or a lack thereof. Some have studied more, some less; some seem to be on leave, and hardly anybody actually walks in perfect step with one another. Each one's relationship is 100 percent private with his commander. The rules apply to all alike, yet in all the differences among men, God's army is united as one. It will be victorious; His Word reigns supreme, and it is a good and beautiful thing.

It is common for people to think that God is off running the universe somewhere and is not concerned with each of us on a personal basis. That was my way of thinking for a very long time. What a difference it is to know, beyond a doubt, that my Jesus is with me and you who believe, and He is always ready to be there for us. How can God be in so many different places at one time, you might ask. Well, the Holy Spirit, which God gives to us at our salvation, is a part of Him that becomes ours to keep, like a rebirth-day present. He says that He will never leave us nor forsake us (Heb.13:5, Amp). His purpose is to glorify God and to guide and help us. There is not the slightest possibility that anyone can ever love us as much or treat us as well as He does, yet I know people who would practically die for their pet or their looks or whatever, and still not give God a second thought. Yet He continues to love us.

There are a number of accounts in the Bible that tell about God's desire for His people to love Him, but they rejected Him instead. It's unbelievable when we look at the whole picture and see that people could think of themselves as so independent and intelligent without God's help that they could live without Him—and even do all right for themselves. Take air, water, food, and gravity, just for starters. Then there's the power of Satan, whose job it is to separate people from God and even to kill us if he can. Satan can only be defeated by and through God's Word, yet people blindly—by choice—stumble along under Satan's whip and control. In most cases, he can do more damage toward the Kingdom of God by keeping Christians in the condition of failure than by actually killing them. If Christians weren't subject to the devil's foul play, then God wouldn't have told us how to deal with him. If we are always negative or receiving only negative results in life while claiming to be Christian, what is appealing about that to unsaved people? The less victorious we are, the greater the testimony that silently speaks, "Most people, including Christians, live with constant struggles and few victories, so it must just be the way things really are." Say "No thanks" to the world with their cooperation with Satan. Say "No thanks" to failure, which was not the reason for our creation. That Adam-and-Eve spirit of disobedience and doubt has multiplied into many misdirected souls, and that is very sad. It amazes me that so few people are willing to really be sold out to God, but instead they go along with a smelly, trouble-causing beast tapping them on from behind. Read the Bible and learn the good news. It really is a healthy, wholesome, great way of life. Let's be on the winning side and arrive at the grand finale ready for a jubilee as joyful, victorious Christians. It's available and waiting.

In Psalm 81, God says that when His people called out to Him in trouble, He delivered them. He brought them out of Egypt and rescued them from bondage. He told them to ask of Him, and He would do it. He was so good to them. Then He said that His people wouldn't listen to Him and would have nothing to do with Him, so He let them go after their own stubborn will. Verses 13–16 (Amp) state, "Oh that My people would listen to Me, that Israel [meaning us too] would walk in My ways! Speedily then I would subdue their enemies, and turn My hand against their adversaries. (Had Israel listened to Me in Egypt, then) those who hated the Lord would come cringing before Him, and their defeat would have lasted forever. God would feed Israel (now) also with the finest of the wheat, and with honey out of the rock would I satisfy you." When "Israel" is referred to, remember that we, as believers in Christ, have been grafted into the tribe of Judah, as His natural lineage was within that tribe (see Heb. 7:14), and we are His children. What a wonderful ancestry to be able to claim!

We turn down so very much when we snub or ignore God. The choice of following after the world and its ways instead of God and His ways will clearly be revealed as disastrous in the afterlife, and probably in this life too. When the flames from the fires of hell surround tormented souls, they will finally get it—but as we've heard a thousand times, it really will be far too late, and it really will be far too hot.

Our choice of Heaven instead of hell should motivate us to want to tell others too. For the people's sake, we must see how important proclaiming the Gospel is. If we don't do it, nobody will.

Please be bold and diligent and try to help folks see the joy and advantages to being a Christian. Satan manipulates the world to try to make Christians seem corny and beneath the people living by his standards, as though we're emotionally unstable and inferior in intellect. It's time to turn the tide now, and don't feel embarrassed. *Merriam-Webster's Dictionary* defines "embarrassed" as to cause to feel self-conscious, confused, ill at ease, disconcerted, or flustered. We can see how destructive to our witness those feelings could be. We can see who causes them and who can cast them down. It's embarrassing to have been so embarrassed so many times! That's my personal story, but thank God, I have learned to let faith and truth lead me on. Every time I go far beyond my comfort zone, I remember the verse in Luke 6:33 (Amp): "And if you are kind and good and do favors to, and benefit those who are kind and good and do favors to and benefit you, what quality of credit and thanks is that to you? For even the preeminently sinful do the same." God knows when it's especially difficult for us to overcome our discomfort in order to serve Him. He knows that the world can be mean and forceful against us. From that point of view, I can rejoice in knowing that by pushing on, we say to our Father, "I really love you." From a broader point of view, think about this:

> **Why in Heaven's name would we be embarrassed over talking about being loved and saved by the God of love and life? The great deceiver has deceived the wrong into thinking they're the right, the right thinking they may be wrong, and going so far as to make the right feel embarrassed over being right. Lord, have mercy on us and help us, please. Let us be crusaders, let us make You glad.**

Let us be strong, willing, and feel honored to be the witnesses we need to be for the God who has given us His love and everlasting life in glory. Do not hide this magnificent miracle, or

27

even consider being shy about it. Go forth and conquer (1 John 5:4, Amp) in Jesus's name. We are on God's side, and He will be victorious—He is on our side. Share that good news with joy. Do somebody a really big favor and help save his or her life.

In reading from Psalms 81, it is hard to understand how our wonderful God could do so much for them and us, yet still be snubbed. It looks like a very sad situation—not only because of the folly we are heading toward, but also for our kind and gracious Father, who desired acknowledgment and love. Often we have felt unappreciated and pushed aside when we have given our all for someone. We know there's no point in trying to force him or her to care, because it just doesn't work that way. God doesn't force anyone either, because it never means the same that way, but He deserves our kindness and love.

In Psalm 78 (Amp), the same kinds of things were going on. "And they (earnestly) remembered that God was their rock, and the Most High God their redeemer. Nevertheless they flattered Him with their mouth, and lied to Him with their tongue. For their heart was not right or sincere with Him, neither were they faithful and steadfast to His covenant. But, He (earnestly) remembered that they were but flesh, a wind that goes and does not return. How often they defied and rebelled against Him in the wilderness and grieved Him in the desert! And time and again they turned back and tempted God, provoking and incensing the Holy One of Israel" (35–41). We can tell by it saying "time and again" that He kept loving them and giving them more chances. However in Luke 8 (Amp), we find the parable of the sower, sowing seed in different types of ground. Verse 12 says, "Those along the traveled road are the people who have heard; then the devil comes and carries away the message out of their hearts, that they may not believe [acknowledge Me as their Savior and devote themselves to Me], and be saved [here and hereafter]." It clearly says that the message was in their hearts for a while. The Bible also says in 1 Peter 4:18 (Amp), "And if the righteous are barely saved, what will become of the godless and wicked?" Christ expects an abiding devotion.

That is not added on after tricking someone to become saved. It is included in the repentance and belief required for salvation. If one has done that according to the true biblical meaning of being born-again, then he or she will not find following Jesus difficult, but will desire to become more like Him.

Matthew Henry's Commentary on the Bible advises that we secure our souls by committing them to God. He further says,

> The best of God's servants, His own household, have so much amiss in them as renders it fit and necessary that God should sometimes correct and punish them with His judgments. Judgments begin at the house of God. Those who are the family of God have their worst in this life—such persons or societies of men as disobey the gospel of God are not of His church and household, though possibly they may make the loudest pretentions. The sufferings of good people in this life are demonstrations of the unspeakable torments that are coming upon the disobedient and unbelieving—the ungodly and the [unrepentant] sinner are unquestionably in a state of damnation.
>
> God is their Creator and has out of mere grace made many kind promises to them of eternal salvation in which He will show Himself faithful and true. When called to believe, obey and to suffer according to the will of God, they should look chiefly to the safety of their souls, which are put into hazard by affliction and cannot be kept secure otherwise than by committing them to God, who will undertake the charge, if they commit them to Him in well-doing.

This requires serious thought. If we, as Christians, are not taught and corrected on earth, then where are we to learn about the walk of faith, obedience, trust, and consequences? It is highly recommended that we quit striving against God. Submit and commit to God any area that we think could affect our being considered a member of the household of God. Matthew Henry's comments sound like Heaven has no place for punishment and that God deals with Christians while they are away from Heaven and are abiding on earth. He also seems to say that if we do not submit and commit our soul to Him while we're here—*before* we expect to return to the homeland of Heaven—then there is nothing more for Him to do with us. We either choose to side with God's way, or we remain on earth and are considered spiritually dead by virtue of our own choice, facing the consequences of that choice. Those who remain are known as the ones who will be left behind. God's proverbial train is only going in one direction. He has offered us the opportunity to board the Heaven-bound train. If we don't choose to go, He has no train going anywhere else. Now, sometimes you may be in a place where His train makes more than one trip past your station, giving you further opportunity—but each time could be the last. Picture how a person behaves in the movies when they have just missed the train at an urgent, important time, and getting somewhere special was like a life-or-death situation to them. That is a clear example of desperation. In the movie you may hope for a plane or bus to rescue the situation, but with God, there is no alternate solution. Those left standing will then realize total despair and complete hopelessness. Consider the glory train, please.

In Philippians 3:11–13 (Amp) Paul says, "That if possible I may attain to the [spiritual and moral] resurrection [that lifts me] out from among the dead [even while in the body]. Not that I have now attained [this ideal] or am already made perfect, but I press on to lay hold of (grasp) and make my own, that for which Christ Jesus, the Messiah, has laid hold of me and made me His own. I do not consider, brethren, that I have captured and made it my own [yet]; but one thing I do—it is my one aspiration; forgetting what lies behind and straining forward to what lies ahead. I press on toward the goal to win the [supreme and heavenly] prize to which God in Christ Jesus is calling us upward." Then Paul advises that believers stick with his example and pattern as to godly living. Continuing in verses 18–20, it says, "For there are many, of whom I have often told you and now tell you even with tears, which walk (live) as enemies of the cross of Christ, the Anointed One. They are doomed and their fate [is] eternal misery (perdition); their god is their stomach (their appetites, their sensuality) and they glory in their shame, siding with earthly things and being of their party, but we are citizens of the state (commonwealth, homeland) which is in Heaven, and from it also we earnestly and patiently await [the coming of) the Lord Jesus Christ, the Messiah, [as] Savior, Who will transform and fashion anew the body of our humiliation to conform to and be like the body of His glory and majesty, by exerting that power which enables Him even to subject everything to Himself."

Most everybody preaching the Gospel today believes that events on earth are now lining up closely with the biblical predictions regarding the end-time. Loving and honoring Him would please His loving, kind heart, as well as keep us out of trouble. It is so easy to get caught up in the cares of this old world. In my imagination, we probably look like an ant hill from Heaven's perspective, except that ants are industrious in a positive way, not a negative one. It's like we are looking through a microscope with one eye closed, while the opened eye is focusing on one little magnified detail (our own set of circumstances, which are constantly changing), and we never look up with both eyes open to see the great, unchanging, holy God of Heaven and earth, beckoning us to come taste and see (Ps. 34:8, Amp) that life in the grander scheme of things is very, very good.

When folks turn Him down or reject Him, they shouldn't blame Him if things don't go so well for them, either in this life or the life hereafter—without Him. It won't be that He doesn't love them, but in order to be fair to all, He has established spiritual laws to which everyone must adhere. There are thousands of promises in the Bible, from God to us. If you have money in the bank but don't realize that it's there, then you obviously won't claim it even if you have a serious need. A promise from God is better than money in the bank, but sincerity in your attitude toward Him is highly recommended. He is not mocked or fooled. People need to get to know Him, give Him honor, and treat Him with great reverence. He is no respecter of persons (Acts 10:34–35, Amp), and what He has done for one He will do for all. We just need to follow the simple directions of John 3:16. The word "believe" in the New Testament always carries commitment and means to adhere to, rely on, and trust in. This is not about believing with your intellect. James 2:19 (Amp) says, "You believe that God is one; you do well. *So do the demons believe* and shudder [in terror and horror such as make a man's hair stand on end and contract the surface of his skin]!" (emphasis added). Obviously *they* aren't saved.

In Isaiah 65:1–3 (Amp) God says, "I was ready to be inquired of by those who asked not; I was to be found by those who sought Me not. I said, Here I am, here I AM to a nation that has not called on My Name. I have spread out My hands all the day to a rebellious people, who walk in a way that is not good, after their own thoughts; a people who provoke me to My face continually."

Picture our God standing on a cloud just above you, saying that His heart is longing for you and that He is ready, hoping, and waiting for you to ask of Him—but you don't ask. He is ready to be found by you, but you don't look to Him. He then says twice, "Here I am—here I am," and He spreads out His hands for a long, long time, waiting for you.

Now, consider this carefully: Have you ever responded to Him with your heart and soul? I am not asking about whether you were water baptized as an infant before you were of an age of accountability. I'm asking whether you were spiritually baptized and were aware of it being a real commitment, and even if you were old enough to know what you were doing, were you possibly just making yourself feel good based on a brief moment of emotion? I am not asking about being confirmed through a religious class. I am asking if you have responsibly said yes to Jesus, accepting Him into your heart as your personal Savior. Only we can say for ourselves if our hearts have remained hard and untouched, or whether a life-changing event occurred through the love of Christ saturating our being in a true spiritual baptism. I am asking whether or not you realize and truly recognize that you have a new life in Christ. This is not about whether or not you have chosen some of the bigger social issues to act morally correct about, simply because it is expected from the Christian or conservative public and you choose to be associated with their views. This is a question about the reality of salvation, which is to have a renewed, repentant, committed-to-Christ change of life and heart. He offers joy, peace, and the miraculous. His love is real. He is real. He is a living being in whose image we are created. He is our Father. He gives us the right to live in Heaven someday, and He knows the human reality that is specifically yours, which is temporal. He is giving you the opportunity to know His reality, which is specifically eternal.

Let's show Him a love called out of our hearts by His preciousness to us, showing it both to Him and the world. Let's not be ashamed of the Gospel. We are in a relationship that is divine and far more spectacular than anything the world has to offer, so why in the world (which barely knows love at all) would we act like we agree with people who think Christians are misguided or misfits. When we allow our denominational differences to override our love for one another, we violate the law of love. Thus, our failure to properly represent Christ damages our credibility and genuineness. I believe the statistics that show Christianity to be on the decline. But however many we are, we could, should, and would be making a showing as dedicated believers if we really took a stand for God and actually presented Him as having power and authority over our lives and our circumstances.

> **The battle between good and evil is raging, so where are all the soldiers of the Lord who should have shown up by now? Where are all the Christians who care enough to take a stand or take a risk? If it's with God, it isn't a risk anyway, and you will have upheld God and the Gospel.**

The devil needs to be resisted (Jas. 4:7, KJV) and defeated, and believers need to show the world that our God reigns. Hurrah for Him, and hurrah for you if you're enlisted in His army as an active member, or if you intend to become one.

There is one thing that I can positively say about following God: "When the roll is called up yonder," I most surely do want to hear my name. I cannot imagine being left standing there with no further opportunity to choose. Heaven forbid!

God bless you, and I love you,
Dian

Chapter Three

Brave Heart

It takes courage to stand against evil and to be brave in the face of trouble, especially when facing our enemy, Satan. We can earn the title of "brave heart" when we have conviction and show faith and strength. "What then shall we say to [all] this? If God be for us, who [can be] against us?—Who can be our foe, if God is on our side?" (Rom. 6:31, Amp). Remember, this is our God who did not withhold or spare His own Son but gave Him up for us. Doesn't that mean to us that our well-being was truly a commitment to Him? God gave Himself for us that we might live.

The emphasis is on the truth, magnificence, and holiness of God, and our desire to obtain as much holiness in our behavior as we can discipline ourselves into, simply because we want to honor Him and be like Him. He is our Father who loves us and is offering us glorious, eternal life in Heaven with Him. The only real holiness that we have comes from the Holy Spirit's presence within us, and the more we allow Him to guide us, the more it shows in our character as a living testimony.

> **Have you ever thought about the number of people who readily say that they expect to live in Heaven someday, seeming to claim a sort of title-deed to the place—yet they never really try to know God or show regard for the one from whom they expect to receive this gift? People just expect salvation to be given to them. If that isn't going right along with the world's way of thinking, what is? We should all know that we do have to know the owner through having faith and obtaining salvation.**

Ephesians 2:8–9 (Amp) is very specific in explaining, "by grace are ye saved through faith," and there are no rituals, decrees, or ordinances—no works of any kind—that can get you in. Verse 10 says that we become "His workmanship, recreated in Christ Jesus, [born-anew]," and verse 12 explains that before being born again, "you were at that time separated (living apart) from all part in Him; utterly estranged and outlawed from the rights of Israel as a nation, and strangers with no share in the sacred compacts of the [Messianic] promise—with no knowledge of or right in God's agreement, His covenants, and you had no hope—no promise; you were in the world without God." One simply cannot obtain the right to Heaven without knowing and believing in Jesus. It must be through faith and salvation. "For God so loved the world that He gave his only begotten Son, that whosoever believeth in Him should not perish, but have everlasting life" (John 3:16, KJV).

When people first come to understand the born-again experience, they begin to study and learn about all the questions and difficulties they previously had in reading and understanding the Bible. One of my own doubts was in not knowing how to be sure that the Bible hadn't been made up by smart, thoughtful, hopeful people. After I became spirit-filled, it was easy to explore my questions because then I trusted God and didn't feel like I might stumble onto a contradiction; I felt comfortable to read and learn and just soak it in. Before that I had wanted to believe it all, but I had a nagging fear that my suspicious mind might lead me to an "ah ha" question, and I really wanted it to be true, though it did sound too good to be. I can cancel all your fears about contradictions by telling you that even if it seems that you may have found something to question, it won't work out in your behalf. You'll just find that God always proves out to be both good and right. People misread and misunderstand things all the time. Just establish it firmly in your thinking that you intend to always give God the benefit of the doubt—that you know that He is incapable of lying and that He will lead you into all truth.

After becoming saved and after learning to be a brave heart, there is usually an increased interest in God, along with many questions. There are great study books available. There are many versions of the Bible that are easy to read and understand, and God wants us to become familiar with Him and His Word. Some of the exceptional books that surround me in my study are listed on the references page at the end of this book. My two favorite books outside of the reference book material is *The Holiest of All* by Andrew Murray, followed by *Smith Wigglesworth—The Complete Collection of His Life Teachings.* I also enjoy every word of *And He Healed Them All,* by Gloria Copeland. Because of having had ownership in Christian bookstores, my library of Christian books is quite extensive and wonderful.

In *God's Plan for Man* by Finis Jennings Dake, there is a lot of supportive information that is good in building a firm foundation. However, one thing that is highly important to stress is that if you don't find what you think of as a rational answer to one of your questions, then just trust God. Don't question Him; He will put it all together for you in due time, but whatever you do, don't act like you know more than He does, and don't doubt Him. Trust Him and go on with your loving, faith-filled desire to learn. You'll be blessed by not questioning Him.

This particular quote is taken from chapter 2 of *God's Plan for Man*. I find it to be extremely practical and thought-provoking support for the validity of our book of life, the Holy Bible.

> The following reasons are sufficient to prove to an unbiased mind that the Bible is an inspired revelation of God: 1. Its Wonderful Unity. Over forty different authors wrote the sixty-six books of the Bible during a period of over 1,800 years; and they all had one theme—the creation and redemption of the human race by God through Jesus Christ and the Holy Spirit.
>
> These books of the Bible were written by men from all walks of life such as kings, priests, judges, lawyers, princes, shepherds, soldiers, courtiers, statesmen, musicians, inventors, singers, poets, preachers, prophets, fishermen, farmers, tentmakers, publicans, physicians, rich men and poor men. They were written in various lands of three continents—Europe, Asia, and Africa. They were written in different ages and by many men, some who never saw each other or knew what the others wrote on the same subjects, yet when their writings became one book, there is not one contradiction among them.
>
> Suppose forty medical men, each in a different land and age, would write forty books on how to cure a disease, what kind of cure would such a collection make? How much unity would one find among their writings? Collect together forty books of man on any subject and one can see many contradictions and controversies among the authors. Some will be found trying to prove how the others are wrong and why his theory is right.

This is all too apparent to those who have read different authors on any one subject. There is no unity of thought between the books of men on any subject. But there is perfect unity between the books of the Bible, which speak of hundreds of subjects in the realm of religion, politics, science, etc. This proves there is one Divine author for all sixty-six books. Who but a Divine author could produce such a work?

This Bible of ours is full of revelation, inspiration, unity, and superiority. It is unequalled in its benefits to men or in the wisdom, truth, and value it provides for us to live by. When you hold your Bible, you are holding onto God, for He clearly says in John 1:1 (Amp), "In the beginning (before all time) was the Word (Christ), and the Word was with God, and the Word was God Himself." Take your Bible more seriously. It's the most important document in the entire world because it contains the will and testament of our holy God.

Hopefully you get a clearer picture of how divine the Bible is, with perfect harmony throughout, especially after seeing the time, distance, and difficulties it took to put the book together. My personal path in pursuit of a faith-filled walk with God led me through much foundational study. *God's Plan for Man* provided me with a great deal of insight.

I have also learned that compromise concerning the Word does not make you neutral—it makes you wrong. In other words, if it says "thou shalt not," then don't try to justify doing it anyway. The laws of the land don't cancel God's laws. His laws were here from before time began, and using the ACLU's opinion does not and cannot change God's laws. The ACLU stands for American Civil Liberties Union, and it often flies in the face of morality and the principles of God. He, however, doesn't have opinions. Everything is extremely well defined and determined by His moral perfection and goodness. He doesn't make mistakes, and

He doesn't change His mind. Christians don't seem to be taking a stand against things that matter to God. Being saved and learning about Him keeps me intent and set against offenses aimed at my faith. I remember the days of not being overly concerned, though. Life wasn't easy, especially without the power of the Holy Spirit.

I remember reading poems to my two little boys, and one of the poems was about the female of the species being more deadly than the male, especially concerning the safety of her babies. I loved my boys more than life, and I know that they knew that, but had I known then what I know now, and had I taught them the same, maybe we could have been spared some of the pitfalls that were so difficult for our family. I am mostly referring to the kinds of things that happen to families and people regularly in a life not fully submitted to God. An example would be in the lack of role models of parents and the lack of correct, nurturing discipline of children and teens, which can have terrible results. Another would be in the many overall family member failures in life due to lack of prayer and faith, from success in school to divorce of the parents. I was then an adult and had the opportunity to change my life through God's Word. God has taught me to learn from my mistakes but not to dwell on guilt or error from the past. If we had been spirit-filled Christian parents, and had we raised our children with the power of the Holy Spirit as a constant presence in our home, who can say what would have happened? Some of the more devastating examples will be given in chapters following. This I do know: parents have a serious responsibility over the little lives that God gives us as our babies, and it's not about whether they get designer shoes and everything else that they want, or whether they make a team or go to the right schools. It's about preparing them for the life they will lead, their ability to make sound, good, godly choices, and how they might rule the land if they grew up to be president. Would they honor the ACLU or Father God?

Most people who don't know much about the Bible really seem to be relatively satisfied with that way of life. Prior to being introduced to my present walk with the Lord, my thinking had been that maybe I knew enough about God to get by, and that the Bible was far too difficult to tackle. Years of sitting in front of a television, plus being brainwashed by the ways and education of the world, had me on a very casual path in life. During my childhood years, I had learned that I was supposed to remember to pray and to say, "Now I lay me down to sleep." I learned how to recite the Pledge of Allegiance and say that I believed in Jesus and was saved by grace. In my teen years I had decided that the way people lived on TV was the way people really lived. That way of thinking developed during the years after I moved away from my granny. From that time on and for nearly thirty years, nothing caused my spiritual understanding to be significantly altered. This is living proof that all churches are not created equal. There were many periods of time during my "dark ages" that I attended churches regularly, but without the power of God being displayed, nothing affected me deeply or awakened me spiritually. Life seemed like such a state of contradiction and confusion. Parents especially should realize that those two states of being still exist for all the children who are seeing a little of Christianity and a lot of worldliness.

To parents who are allowing their children to grow up this way, more or less just sharing your living quarters with you without godly guidelines, let me lovingly say: You are not helping our world to be a better place, or helping your children to know the joy and blessings of God. Without structured moral behavior as a way of life, they are being deprived of both giving and receiving the good things of life. Teaching them to become moral individuals with admirable character is teaching them to live life with an undefeatable strength—with the will and determination to help defeat evil (as the power and Word of God gives us instructions and the right to do). It teaches us not to contribute to evil—and to stand with personal strength and conviction against it, and to truly be a brave heart.

Being brave can be especially difficult at times. Teenagers may have the greatest struggles because they haven't had time to become spiritually mature, and there is so much pressure from every direction. Those years are the early stages of coming face-to-face with the conflict between good and evil in the grown-up world, and if there is no one to intercede on their behalf, their souls can be put off course for the rest of their lives. If they are not taught Christianity by example in their home, where God says they are to be trained up in the way that they should go (Prov. 22:6, KJV), then warning signs flash. They may never again be in the path of a person who will be an effective witness.

At a very young age I was sent to live with my granny in a tiny community called Enville, Tennessee. I had never lived where there had been a television, and there was no TV at her house—no booze, no late nights out, no arguing, cursing, or lies. It was peaceful, and there were clear guidelines. She could play any instrument by ear and sang hymns all the time. We had a wonderful garden and canned everything for winter. She let me churn the butter or turn the ice-cream crank, but I wasn't much help at making soap or salting down the hams to hang in the smokehouse for winter. Going to another family's farm to see molasses being made was a festive day, and just so I would know about a variety of things, she actually took me raccoon hunting one night. That hunt required a kerosene lantern and our going into the dark forest. Because we serve such an awesome God, we actually found a raccoon sitting on the lower limb of a big tree, with his eyes glowing yellow and looking frightful. We had no way of catching him (which she had obviously known all along), but finding him and his glowing eyes, along with the shadows and sounds among the big trees, made it a very exciting event. There was just enough of a twinge of scariness in the darkness that night to make a perfect childhood memory. An all-day singing and dinner on the ground was a major event, and a ride in someone's wagon was always fun. If she went to the cotton fields to pick cotton, so did I, and I did my part with a challenge in my heart, because each pound meant more earnings. There's not one thing in that lifestyle that disturbed my conscience or was confusing, then or now. I cherish those years and consider their influence on my life to be the anchor that held me afloat before I really understood about a personal walk with Jesus. It was wonderful, and I was growing up to be a well-guided girl. I had any baby animal around that I wanted for a pet, took piano lessons, and learned to do embroidery and to climb trees. America was the grandest, most honored country, so generous, beautiful, and good from sea to shining sea. I learned by example, seeing and behaving with never a mention of an alternate set of values. We were very poor, and I had no idea of it. To me, it was as God said in Genesis: "and it was good."

My life was about to take a road toward a whole new world and go from one with structure and direction to one with a serious lack of both. It was almost like a baby octopus trying to swim both east and west. At thirteen years of age, I had been taken from my granny's home in rural Tennessee and moved to a new home in Memphis with another family member. The TV lifestyle of glamour, parties, alcohol, and an overall different way of life was the way my new family lived. It looked the same as the TV people, so I decided that my country upbringing had really been lacking and that now I had the chance to live a normal life. I had to make some changes fast, as I certainly didn't fit in.

When I think about those changes in my life that I had to adjust to at that age—in going from a simple, country, Christian way to a diabolically different citified life—it is truly a wonder that I survived. I know that the experiences of life have helped make me who I am today, but like a message in a bottle, I bobbed around in some dangerous waters. I had my first drink of alcohol that first year. I had far too many opportunities to make my own decisions, with basically no guidance and no one paying any attention to what I was doing. I struggled to be liked by my peers and to not be thought of as too backward by the adults. Naturally, I received mockery from both groups at times. I no longer felt any kind of nurturing love—just a struggle to maintain some sort of balance between the values that had been instilled in me during earlier years and the new value system of appearance, acceptance, being popular, and having fun. After trimming down during the first year, I remember being told not to worry, but "the little girls wouldn't like me because the little boys would." Now there's a sound approach for a young girl to feel comforted by. I wanted to feel loved and to be valued the way I had been before, to be a person with self-esteem. I didn't have that again for a very long time, though I tried. Before I was nineteen years old, I had several boys propose to me, and I accepted most every one of them (though none of it was of a serious nature), but how disturbing is that!

The closest that I really got to a church during that time was to go a couple of times with different friends. One was Catholic, so I considered becoming Catholic. Another was Jewish, so I considered becoming Jewish. You can see that I was left to figure it out for myself. I had never even heard of being filled with the Holy Spirit. I had heard of the Holy Ghost, but without any details that I can recall. What would have become of me, had it not been for the Lord?

Allow me a brief period of explanation about the term "spirit filled." First of all, all people who are born-again have the Holy Spirit (same as Holy Ghost) within them, as do the ministries of the church and those people are no less born again than another. However, we are faced with the question in Acts 19:2 (KJV): "Have ye received the Holy Ghost since ye believed?" Luke 11:13 explains that the Father will give the Holy Spirit to those who ask. John 20:22 says that Jesus breathed on them and said to them, "Receive ye the Holy Ghost." He comes to those who seek Him. Receiving the Holy Spirit brings about a new, more intensive walk with God. You want to yield your complete person to show the love of God as it pours forth. A divine power is now dwelling within you. You feel spiritually energized, warmed, and encouraged by it. Your mind is clearer, your excitement is higher, and your physical being joyfully participates in active worship. He is a wonder-making, power-producing member of the Holy Trinity, and once you have His Spirit indwelling you, you will never let Him go. It seems extreme to those who are unaccustomed to the idea, but it is very biblical, brings renewed integrity and strength to the believer, and is definitely worth pursuing. I would give up my life before I would give Him up, and He is a highly recommended guide and comforter to seek after. Don't be held back by others' opinions. Read, seek, receive, live—and then tell the discouragers about Him too. You will never be the same after being fulfilled in such a spiritually wholesome, wonderful way.

Nearly thirty years later, after leaving my granny's home, I became a spirit-filled Christian. I will not attempt to justify or count the sins of my life, but when I say I can relate to other people's guilt and sin, believe me, it's true. However, like my pastor says, "let us not be trying to raise the dead" regarding our past. I am through with it, I have repented for it, Jesus's blood has covered it, and He says He has forgotten it, so it is no more. And isn't that a lovely thing to be able to say! However, for the sake of giving more personal information regarding the testimony of how great God's grace really is, I need to be more specific. Galatians 5:19–21 lists the works of the flesh (human nature apart from God) as adultery, fornication, uncleanness, lewdness, idolatry, sorcery, hatred, contentions, jealousies, outbursts of wrath, selfish ambition, dissensions, heresies, envy, murders, drunkenness, revelries, and the like, and it says that those who practice such things will not inherit the Kingdom of God. With great shame and a humble and contrite heart, I appealed to God to forgive me for the things on that list with which I could identify. He did. In a very deep and personal place in your heart, ask yourself how many of those things you can identify with, at least somewhat in your life now. During the thirty years before becoming spirit filled, I could have identified with several. There are no good things on that list. They are all bad and they all bring miserable consequences. Just look at them again to see how any one of those things could bring misery to you or to someone you know and love, if you are living with worldly ways instead of living for God.

If your life includes any of these things now, and if you have a conscience at all, you live with guilt and shame. If you don't have a conscience about sin, you could still suffer terrible consequences simply because a worldly lifestyle puts you much more in harm's way. Jealousy, rage, drunkenness, murder, sexually transmitted diseases, and evil of all sorts swarm and swirl around that list of sins. This statement may or may not apply to your life, but it is an example of the other side of living a Godly life, and I saw examples of many of those demon-induced threats to my life.

Look at the young woman on the front of this book and think about what you see in her face. What I see is what I know to have been there. I see kindness and hope that love and goodness still exists and can be found somewhere, someday. It is absolutely true that I have nearly always been kind, I have nearly always been forgiving, and I never intended to hurt anyone. I wanted to be loved and to have a sweet, good life. Because my mother was intent on climbing the social ladder, I can say to her credit that I was not allowed to dress in any other way than like a lady. She and my step father would not allow me to have friends that they considered tramps or tacky. It was for the sake of appearances, but it served a good purpose for me. I still had a great deal of my granny's influence in my soul, so I was not a "bad girl." Those were days when the entire family was shamed if a young girl became pregnant, and it was not a common thing among teens—at least not the people who I knew—for there to be actual sex. There was a different code of ethics then. I wish there was still.

My first huge mistake was to marry my high school sweetheart. He had graduated from Central High in Memphis a year before me, joined the army, and was then stationed in Germany. We had previously broken up, and I had not heard from him for two years when we started writing to each other. He asked me to come to Germany to marry him. I was nineteen years old and he was twenty-one. I lived with my mother, who was divorced for the third time, and my younger half-sister. I hardly knew my dad because he and my mom divorced while I was still a baby. My mother was either at work or a social event most all the time, and my dear little sister, Marsha, called me Mama for a few years. On the day that I received his proposal by mail, I had gone into my mother's bedroom, sat down on the side of her bed, and told her that Jay had asked me to fly to Germany to marry him, and then I asked her what she thought about the idea. After only a moment she said, "Well, Dian, even if you have to divorce him after a year, it would be worth it to see Europe." So on that sound advice, I applied for my passport and arrived in Munich, Germany, in a blizzard in January 1959. I had been going to modeling school in Memphis—those were the days of the Marilyn Monroe figure— and my youthful, hopeful ego had me convinced that with the positive qualities I did have, he would absolutely love, adore, and cherish me, and we would live happily ever after. At this point in my life, I had lived with an aunt, first one granny then the other, and my mother with two different husbands other than my dad. I had seen another baby half-sister allowed to live with her father's family and then disappear out of my life, and I had an alcoholic, unavailable father. But now I was finally finding a secure, loving new home—or so I thought.

The first clue that should have sent me packing was finding his dog tags on the kitchen table with atheist listed as his religion. I was shocked and worried, because even without church being an active part of my life at that time, I still had the basics from my granny and certainly knew that atheism was not okay and that people were supposed to believe in God. He said that he hadn't believed in God since his father had died three years before. I am reminded of a recent quote that I saw: "If I don't believe in atheists, does that mean they don't exist?"

The other situation that really added to the undoing of our relationship—which hadn't been done properly to begin with— was that my anticipation regarding the intimate part of our lives had been based solely on romantic movies. There was Cary Grant and Clark Gable, Audrey Hepburn and Gene Tierney. Most everything was left to the imagination, and romance was about beautiful people with beautiful lives. My life became considerably different from that. I was neither cherished nor adored. Jay was an introvert, didn't like to socialize, and said he didn't like ugly people because it made him uncomfortable to look at them. I don't remember even knowing anyone that I thought qualified for that prejudice. He would be embarrassed if I tried to hold hands with him in public, and worst of all, the bedroom was a sort of torment to him because he would not tolerate either being seen without clothes on, or seeing me unclothed. He would not even look at the body that I had thought he as my husband would love. He made me feel ashamed and afraid that he would be angry with me, and I became very self-conscious. We were married fifteen months, and my first baby, Scott, was six months old, before we ever saw each other without clothes on. By that time, he had destroyed all interest that I could have had, and we did not have God to see us through such an emotionally charged tangle of distrust and resentment. Love for me had not been very successful. Scottie was about eight months old when, in anger, Jay rubbed Scottie's face in vomit to "teach him a lesson." The anger and hate that I felt toward him over that still stirs in me when I remember it. After the initial recollection and immediate emotional response, grace moves in and allows me to be the kind of woman that I know God wants me to be.

When my two little boys were one and three years old, Jay had a prostitute with him in our new home and in our bed while I was en route from Memphis, Tennessee, with the boys. We were on a three-day trip going halfway around the world to join him in his new assignment in Bangkok, Thailand. After that episode there was no turning back on my disrespect and dislike for him. I would go to different churches from time to time after we returned to the United States, sometimes crying so hard that I wouldn't go to that church again because of embarrassment. At different times I would make an effort to reconcile with Jay, and we both would make a halfhearted try for a while. He would not go to church with me, and I would ask why we couldn't just go to a movie and out to dinner, but he always wanted to drink and party and would hurtfully tell me that I was no fun if I didn't drink too, so I did. He also liked to say to me, "Nothing is useless—it can always be used as a bad example." Life didn't get any better. Our personal relationship was not good, and he was often mean to all of us.

We lived in different countries all over the world, spending a total of fifteen years out of the United States. Nine of them were consecutive. I adjusted to a loveless marriage and partied with the crowd. I guess we were drinking and dancing across the globe like people who didn't seem to have a care in the world, because Jay wasn't looking for anything more and I had settled for what I did have as being all there was. I did not know, nor am I aware of having met, a spirit-filled Christian in any of our travels. Any family connections that I had previously had seemed distant and remote. Both my grannies had died during those years of our travels.

Seven consecutive years were spent in England. I went to church regularly there on the military base and took Scott and Greg with me. Jay still wouldn't go. On Saturday nights, he and I went to the club on base, drank, danced, told jokes, flirted, and didn't seem to notice that God wasn't with us. Believe it or not, I was actually on the church board as social director. The pastor was kind, but his spiritual range appeared to be limited to nice little feel-good, fifteen-minute speeches in a military chapel. That did not seem odd to me, though, because nearly all churches that I had attended seemed to be the same way. Most of the people that we went to church with were also at the club on Saturday night. No one seemed to take God too seriously or share about Him or His life-changing power. The recurring backaches that Jay lived with didn't seem to bother him on Saturday nights.

During the last ten years with him, he had become physically violent and had hit me repeatedly on several different occasions. The last time it happened, he was in a drunken rage after we had been to a party. It was by far the worst of all. When he went for his gun, I left the house and called the police, who called the fire department to break into the house because I had no key and the door was locked. What a terrible commotion, and such an embarrassment. Jay had taken several pills and was unconscious, which then required the ambulance to come. You cannot believe how difficult it was for me to go to the hospital and be in attendance as his wife. I could hear horrible sounds from the pumping out of his stomach. Finally they told me that I could go in to see him, which I did not want to do but respectfully did. I was only in there a few minutes before he took my hand, and then he made a gesture that referred to physical intimacy. I knew then that he had taken the pills to try to manipulate me into feeling sorry for him. It was disgusting to me; I no longer felt obliged to remain at the hospital with him because he was over the worst of it and was recovering. I wasn't.

When I left that time, it was finally over after twenty-two years. I moved into an apartment with another young woman who had recently left her husband too. We shared the two-bedroom apartment until I married Mr. Ralph, one year later. I still had my job with the defense department. Jay did not have extra money to help me with, and I did not ask for half of his retirement income, which I could have had when he retired. When he died, around 2007, he had nothing designated for either Greg or Greg's two little girls, Rebecca and Tylan Grace, his own granddaughters. Even though he was living very comfortably in a pricey condo on the beach in Florida and was reported to have been living well, I believe that he continued to try to punish me through those I loved. All was left to his third wife, who was independently well off when he married her. Greg was hurt deeply because he had never really understood the depth of selfishness that was in his dad's heart before that. In Scottie's case, before Scottie died in 1994, Jay refused to speak with him on the phone—for the same reason, I expect. Scottie was devastated; he was ill and so sad, crying from the pain of it all. I must now say, though, that I honestly would go through those years with Jay all over again if my refusal meant not having my two awesome, wonderful sons.

Scott and Greg—such precious, handsome, bright young men they turned out to be. We were great friends and companions. Scott was the studious, serious one and Greg was lighthearted and happy. When we lived in Mexico City, they both earned money teaching music, Scott the piano and Greg the guitar. At that time, Scott was in the twelfth grade and Greg was in the eleventh. Who knows how different their lives would have been if their parents has been spirit-filled Christians. The only time that they attempted to get out of control was when they were in their late teens to early twenties, and that even happens in Christian families sometimes too. At least it was temporary, and they both became Christians later in life. Once, before Scottie died, he said to me, "Mom, I am not afraid of dying and I know that I am going to be with Jesus, but I just hate to leave you to look after Mr. Ralph alone."

Greg stepped up for that responsibility and did it cheerfully. He now has an exceptional family. We all go to church together, and Greg plays music on the praise and worship team. Brandy, his precious, extraordinary wife, helps at church with the children, who are on the Bible quiz team. None of us are shy about praying together, and talking about the Word is one of our favorite things. It is interesting and exciting when you know that God is real. We always have Sunday lunch together and live in the same neighborhood in a lake community in West Tennessee. We are in and out of each other's homes all the time. We really enjoy belonging to the family of God and to each other. Loving and honoring God puts a whole new environment around a family. It's a special feeling that seems like a comforting cocoon. The life of the family that we had with Jay was disconnected, filled with strife, and it was usually uncomfortable. It was not a feeling of being secure or of the situation ever being stable.

I can analyze the mistakes I made as a young adult, but I don't excuse any of it. I just wish that I had had a personal relationship with God a lot sooner than I did. I had absolutely no idea about really knowing Him. My needs were sometimes just to have someone to talk to me, to offer encouragement and emotional support, or to just be my friend. God would have been all of that and more, and the problems might have been solved.

We can know about and keep the core of moral behavior in our souls, but without having a personal relationship with the living God, our own lack of strength, linked with our lack of knowledge, will give Satan easy access to us. Our family suffered severe destruction. I considered myself to be, and yearned to be, a Christian. However, I also thought that nearly everyone was a Christian because when I had lived in Enville, Tennessee, in earlier years, people seemed to behave with a more serious approach toward Heaven and hell. Adultery, homosexual behavior, lies, lack of honor, and even divorce were seldom heard of in a small rural community then. The faults they may have had weren't obvious to me because I was a child.

I knew in my heart and soul that there was more to God than what I knew about. In later years, no concerned Christian sensed and then responded to my emotional emptiness, or offered me the reality of a daily, personal walk with Christ. No one recommended anything other than what I already had—which was hanging by a thread. None of the churches that I attended through those years offered more than what I had grown up seeing: hymns, silence, respect in the sanctuary, serious looks on everybody's faces, condemnation if you were found out in any wrong activity—as though you were unique in your relationship to sin. During my adult years, I knew that others weren't being perfect because I had heard them gossip and criticize others, and I was aware of all sorts of hypocritical issues that were going on. During the same time that I was aware of sins among the congregation, I also felt that I was sitting among the Gospel police. It was all very confusing. Like so many others, I found it difficult to understand the Bible or to see much more from the Christians than to believe in God and Jesus and to try to be good. I did both, but I just didn't get it.

In judging myself, when considering my very worst sins during the time before I became spirit filled, my answer would have to be not forgiving others of the deep emotional wounds I suffered. I had so many people to forgive for abandonment, loneliness, rejection, and pain. I felt so unloved by the world, except for Scott and Greg. Regarding hate, I could probably equate it with murder if we go by what is in our heart. "Anyone who (abominates, detests) hates his brother [in Christ] is [at heart] a murderer and you know that no murderer has eternal life abiding (persevering) within him" (1 John 3:15, Amp). Even though I still feel an initial stab of pain when I think about how Jay treated me and my children, I have now forgiven him. I have learned to separate the deed from the person, to see that the deed is all that I have the right to condemn. I am so grateful to God for forgiving me. He says that He forgets our offenses when we are humble and sincere in asking His forgiveness. I do not allow those two power twins of Satan (hate and not forgiving) to invade my mind or soul any longer. Most of my worst sins were in reaction to the desperation I felt. What a relief to be rid of the spirit of desperation. What a freedom, what an awesome blessing to no longer feel driven by any of those forces.

In Philippians 3:13 (Amp), Paul says that his one aspiration is in forgetting what lies behind and straining forward to what lies ahead. Then he says he presses on toward the supreme and heavenly prize to which God in Christ Jesus is calling us upward. We know from Paul's life that repentance and the blood of Jesus can make us clean. I will not lie and say that my life has been sin free regarding sexual sin. I thank God for His forgiveness. I am so grateful to have lived beyond the days of that kind of sin so that I could genuinely repent and receive God's mercy. Being honest is not too difficult, but thinking about offending the Lord breaks my heart all over again. The greatest relief is to know that He looks at me through the eyes of love, and He tells all of us that He forgives the offenses when we come to Him with a contrite and humble heart in true repentance. I went through a period of time when I would have preferred death to the grief of regret. It made me understand repentance more fully. Instead of just trying to obtain a pardon for the offense for my own future's sake, my heart was breaking because the offense was against my dear and precious Father. Perhaps the refining power of such guilt and grief taught me more about tenderness and appreciation for the heart of the Father.

The past is the past, and God has cleared my record, which He does on a regular basis for anyone who comes to Him. No one lives a totally sin-free life because of the nature of our birth as human beings, and even though as Christians we don't want to sin, sometimes we still will. But I want to assure you that even if we have done the worst things imaginable, He will still forgive us when we truly repent. Our sins are covered by the blood of Jesus, but we still need to ask for forgiveness and mean it. The Lord's Prayer is our example of a daily prayer, and it asks every day for God to forgive us for our trespasses as we forgive those who trespass against us. We can't out-sin God's grace; only a God like ours could stick with us through so many wrong decisions and still count us as His children, encouraging us to be holy as He is holy, and wanting us to love Him as our Father and friend. There is deep regret for the sins of my past, but as much as I possibly can, I have made things right with everybody involved. My life today is in absolute contrast to the person that I allowed myself to be on different occasions in past times. Trial and error can teach us, if we are willing to be taught. When your remorse is great, you learn to avoid the cause of it—which to a Christian is anything that offends our heavenly Father. My wonderful, forgiving God is real. Every day is a new beginning and a new opportunity to serve Him with my best effort. He knows my heart; He knows the real me. He loves and accepts me, and with all my heart I thank and love God for that. I am also truly grateful that His teaching me the way toward holiness blesses not only my spirit but also my human existence in all areas of life.

God is love, and if you love Him, it shows; it doesn't mean that you love just Him, because He is easy to love, but you must also love everybody, including the mean, the selfish, and the ugly-acting, as He does, which is not so easy to do. He challenges us to meet the needs of others by telling us in Luke 5:33 (Amp), "And if you are kind and good and do favors to and benefit those who are kind and good and do favors to and benefit you, what quality of credit and thanks is that to you? For even the preeminently sinful do the same." We need to go beyond the world's ways in order to be credible Christians, and in the long run we end up being the ones with the blessings because we tried, so it's a win-win situation. Within our willingness lies the value to Him—and our willingness toward Him is what I hope to inspire and encourage within more hearts.

Even without my experiences being told in detail, people certainly can see and know that misery and emotional distress is produced in a life without God's daily influence. What it produces is a product from hell, because Satan has worldly control. We need to start seeing *everything* in the light of good and evil, blessing or cursing. When it's time to step forth with a brave heart, then please be brave. God is with you. Care enough to act accordingly. There is protection under the shadow of the Almighty (see Ps. 91). It cannot be stressed enough that there is a life-changing difference that makes one so much happier, more peaceful, and in ownership of positive faith and hope, in place of hopelessness and despair.

Do you ever wonder though, that if the Holy Spirit and the power He imparts is a reality in people's lives, why don't they let it show? People who have Him love seeing Him in action. For years now, I have observed a lack of interest when conversations turn to God or religion. Maybe that's one reason I got so off course. I sometimes make remarks that sound like I may have been a really terrible person, but when people are serious about their relationship with Jesus, then any wrong spirit within themselves alerts their attention. My personal standards have become high. I only judge myself with diligence because I know that I can always do better, and I do take responsibility for my own mistakes. Consequently, I have learned that avoiding them is far better than having to judge my own sins. When I was in my younger years, few of the people who were supposed to know about Him really knew, or else they would have been willing to talk about Him. People like to claim a lot of privacy about their relationship with God. I guess that's a good way to try to hide the fact that they don't know much to say on the subject, because I have learned that folks who really love God also really love talking about Him.

The testimony of who I am and what has been accomplished because of my relationship and trust in God is descriptive of the opposing forces of good and evil. From an innocent, good beginning as a child, to knowledgeable worldliness, and back into the arms of love and forgiveness—seems to be the pattern many of us take. As with the children of Israel in the wilderness, I had to make many trips around the mountain before getting sight of the promise land.

I want to stay honest and humble before you and to present my hope for all of us to have a stronger, better tomorrow, and a powerful, joyful relationship with God. He is the light of the world; He is the answer to satisfy all our needs, both now and in the future. He has given me blessings beyond belief; an interesting and good life with Him, success, hope, a way to Heaven, and security and joy. Life with Him puts my feet on solid ground. Those sins in my past were done in a pitiful effort to survive or try to hold on in whatever situation I was in. For all of my life, God's offer of love, joy, peace, long suffering, kindness, goodness, faithfulness, gentleness, and self-control (Gal. 5:22–23) were available to me. Those are the things that really fill our hearts' desires, bringing peace and comfort to the wounded soul. Those are the things that demonstrate the likeness of the nature of Christ in a recreated, born-again soul. Those are the things that are truly worth having.

We could really serve mankind well if we would rev it up and enlist some Christian soldiers to march with us in the army of the Lord. We need to look for the people who are struggling in that in-between area and who think that fitting in will get them the acceptance they yearn for—but unfortunately it won't. From one who has been there, I can truly tell you that the world is never satisfied with you. It's really all about Him and our recognizing and honoring Him—and doing our job with joy and enthusiasm toward getting more souls saved. Believe it or not, the focus comes off of you; that's when you really have some peace in your heart, some confidence and contentment in your soul and it is truly the only thing that brings that soul satisfaction! And the good news added to that is that it is a delightful, happy way to live. What's more, one day you will just wake up and realize that God really does love you, that you have extraordinary value to Him, and that you just really aren't all that bad after all. Then you smile from the inside out, realizing that love has released you from worrying about how the world is treating you at times, and you go on about your Father's business still smiling and feeling peaceful. Don't stay in the middle; move into the realm of the full and rich spiritual life, and don't even consider allowing anyone to convince you otherwise. If they try, it will be because they don't have it or understand it, and they most certainly are not qualified to judge it. They have just presented you with someone else (themselves) to convince of the good things of God. Once you've got it, don't let it go. Live it, love it, and thank God for it. Understand that your salvation also includes healing and deliverance.

Remember Psalm 23 (Amp), which says in verses 4–5, "Yes, though I walk through the (deep, sunless) valley of the shadow of death, I will fear or dread no evil; for You are with me; Your rod (to protect) and Your staff (to guide), they comfort me. You prepare a table before me in the presence of my enemies; You anoint my head with oil; my (brimming) cup runs over."

There are two key thoughts that I would like to point out. Verse 4 says, "I walk *through*," which means you aren't staying there, in one place. Verse 5 says, "You prepare a table before me in the presence of my enemies." Well, this is truly good news, because we will have no enemies in Heaven. That promise, then, has to apply to being in this present life and to our being well provided for here—without fear. Thank You, Father God.

> **God is with us, and His Word guides us. We are armed, and we need to march against the gates of hell, which cannot prevail against God's church (Matt. 16:18, KJV). We are not the little church in the vale through whose gates hell is bursting. We are the army of the Lord and are the aggressors.**

Let's get a few victories under our belts, get our courage up, and bring it on home—hallelujah to the Lamb of God who sits upon the throne. If we could just get past ourselves, accept God for His Word, and get on with doing our duty as serious Christians, then things would improve in a hurry, and we'd be happier people for it—with a lot more folks headed for Heaven instead of hell.

It would be so grand if we could get enthusiastic about our good and gracious God! We're all on the same side, learning to focus on our righteous leader. Let's follow Him and truly be His church and His army. Let's start marching and stop holding back. If we really trust God, we won't be ashamed or afraid. Let's march shoulder to shoulder, with our heads up and a song in our heart, as He wants us to do, knowing we are on the winning side. He has given us knowledge, weapons, and faith and assured us of our victory. See Ephesians 6:10–17 (KJV) for the full armor of God and what force it provides against evil. Yes, be very well assured, God's side will win, and that's a victory that I definitely don't want to be left out of. "Who is he that overcometh the world, but he that believeth that Jesus is the Son of God" (1 John 5:5, KJV). I expect you would like to be a part of this great event too!

He is the mighty Creator of our entire universe—there's nothing He can't do.
Who wouldn't follow such a leader—and He wants me and you.
Our horses are named Courage and No Compromise, and we're in this to win,

So Satan, fall the first time, because we don't want
to pierce you again.

So take note, you who want to go, and get up on
your steed.

There are souls out there that need to be won
And delivered over to God's only son.

He's waiting, but not for long.

This is your chance to show God that you really appreciate
and trust Him. If you don't, I can assure you the last fate will
be worse than the first, for the first is going to be a heavenly
celebration! So consider your own best interest, bring some other
folks along, and come on!

> Our battle cry should be "Lord, we're marching
> on."
> And thanks to your weapons of warfare, we aren't
> fighting alone!
> Make way; make way for the army of the Lord;
> We are lifted up—we are not down trod.
> There's victory all about us—we knew it'd end
> this way.
> The Lord has led us onward, and we're heading
> home to stay.
> Be thrilled, brave heart, for you have travelled
> far.
> Your reward, brave heart, is to kiss the face of
> God.

Now go forth and conquer, in Jesus's name. Amen, dear
Jesus—so let it be.

Love,
Dian

Chapter Four

What Does Being a Christian Mean to Me?

In the beginning was God. He is the Alpha and Omega, the First and the Last.

He inhabits the praises of His people. Let praises to Him be declared from cover to cover, and may He be with us all in this journal of Godly encouragement and hope. Amen.

I will attempt to answer the question of what being a Christian means to me. It's too great a task for me to find mere human words with which to answer, and I am overwhelmed by the thought. Let me write my answer to the Lord, who also reads the sincerity of my heart. I fervently pray that my answer can convey the profound sincerity of my heart to you, too. My love and commitment are expressed in part here, and then continued near the end of the book in chapter 12.

I want to praise Him in the high places, praise Him in the low places. I want to stay really close to Jesus and to always trust Him with everything—no matter what! I want to stay right with Him in the face of every adversity, to stay strong. I have failed at times and feel ashamed and sad. He so kindly offers us forgiveness and restores our self-esteem, which derives its very value from His indwelling presence within us. I never want to disrespect His precious blood, shed to make everything good for us. He puts us in right standing again and again.

Father and Lord, please lift me out of worldly thinking and help me to express through my life the importance of knowing You personally and being saved from the fires of hell. Before I knew You well, I was living under many negative and insecure ways. My church background had never impressed Your truth on my heart. When bad things happened to me in life, I would fall on my face and cry and beg and pray, and You always brought me through. Then I would go back to the same drifting spirit, highs and lows, never certain of anything in life—until your precious Holy Spirit descended upon me!

Oh merciful Jesus, Lord and Savior, magnificent Father, light of the world—I am in awe and give praise to my King! I lived in a dark room in my mind; Your Spirit flooded it with glory, truth, and light. I understood then that You are my Father and ever-present friend, my Lord, most holy yet tender and near. Your royal authority gives me high privileges and rights. You make me clean through your righteousness; You give me the right to live as a child of the holy living God, the God who spoke Heaven and earth into existence with a word. Then You gave me Your Word, which continues to speak things into existence and is, in itself, alive and full of power—it is part of you and is called holy. You give me the right to use Your holy Word to rebuke the devil, to live in prosperity and joy. You taught me to love. You make everything good and fill my heart with song. You are wonderful, merciful, and kind. You are my God, my Savior, my conscience, my guide, my answer, my strength, my King. You are what I long for and live for, and You offer me Heaven as my home forever. I love You, Father. I thank You for your precious Holy Spirit, and I praise You in Jesus's mighty name—the Name—that, when used in faith, provides all of the authority and power that created the universe way back then, and that is always waiting for faith to touch and activate it again.

It is my heart's desire that God be loved, praised, and honored. It is my heart's deepest desire apart from seeing Him in person, to tell of His goodness and worth. People should behave in a loving and honorable way toward Him because of who He is; they should openly declare His wondrous ways to the entire world. The reward is far greater than material things.

Salvation alone, even without extra benefits and blessings, is cause enough for us to give all the joy and gratitude that is possible for us to give. Salvation should thrill our souls, even without considering the abundance of blessings He gives, including the right to use the teachings of the Bible on how to pray for additional and constant requests. If He was bombarded with even half as much praise as He receives in requests for more, He would surely be glad, indeed.

God is pure. God is perfect. He has no needs, no ego problems. The praise we offer benefits us because He inhabits the praises of His people; we get the blessing. The Bible says that He is looking for a peculiar people (not peculiar in a strange way, but by being "set apart" for Him by their own choice), a people who can see the value in an invitation to paradise by a pure and holy, all-powerful God. "Who gave himself for us, that he might redeem us from all iniquity, and purify unto himself a peculiar people, zealous of good works" (Titus 2:14, KJV). He isn't concerned with Himself when He calls for praise; He's watching us to see who truly does value and appreciate Him, and who has even a glimpse of the reality of what will take place when we physically die. It's like hoping that your child makes an A. He's still looking for those "set apart" people. He is blessed when His children trust and obey.

Our ego and our pride have imprisoned us in a praise-resistant, near-trance condition. Most people seem to be sitting, standing, or staring with no smile and no movement in response to God. Enemy spirits cause us to be like actors on the stage of life, which will not benefit us when we step out of this life and into the next. Think about the life hereafter, and there will be one. Compare Heaven to hell; doesn't that make you love the idea of Heaven and God enough to be genuinely thankful, and to joyfully show it? Well, that's where praise comes in—both in private and in a crowd. You aren't being asked to praise; you're being given the opportunity to.

Please don't think that I am too intense—think that I am not intense enough! This is about breaking free from the bondage of being unduly inhibited in the presence of God while surrounded by other humans. It's about being wonderfully uninhibited (within the true bounds of decency and order) with your destiny, moving upward and in your favor, before our Lord and King. It's all about later, but we need to fix things now so that we'll be ready when later comes—in case it comes today. So let's rejoice and show God that we value Him and His priceless offer of a glorious, heavenly home. Let's praise Him with love and enthusiasm!

First, we need to make sure that we belong to Him. Contemplate your own salvation and make sure you get it right. There is a warning here, because many are under the false impression that they are saved because: (1) a "holy" *man* said so; Matthew 23:9 (Amp) says to call no man in the church or on earth father, for you have one Father, who is in Heaven; or (2) because of having been water baptized without the necessary spiritual change becoming evident in them; baptism alone does not save a person. In 1 Corinthians 1:14–17, the apostle Paul says that he thanks God that he baptized none of them, except a very few, because Christ sent him not to baptize but to preach the Gospel. In verse 18, he says why. The preaching of the Cross is foolishness to those who aren't saved, "but to those who are *saved, it is the manifestation of the power of God*" (emphasis added). After accepting the doctrine of Jesus, water baptism is important and recommended for all saved people; however it should not be emphasized so that it appears to be the way to salvation. The preaching of the Cross, and the Cross alone, holds the power of God through the death of His Son as the only way to salvation. Repentance and remission of sins always occur *before* baptism, not because of it. Jesus said in Mark 1:15 (KJV), "And saying, the time is fulfilled, and the Kingdom of God is at hand; repent ye, and believe the gospel." There are many instances where Jesus forgave sins without water baptism (a few examples are recorded in Matt. 9:1–7, Luke 7:36–50, Luke18:9–14, and John 4:49–53).

Stop being judgmental and pulling yourselves down—while thinking that you are pulling down the ones you are judging, which you think will elevate you above them. Jesus spoke strongly to the Pharisees about that way of thinking. The marks of a Pharisee are described in Matthew 23 (Amp). Folks who are holding so aggressively to an issue in their (man's) doctrine when "God has offered salvation based on the Gospel message of proclaiming, receiving and accepting the message as a rebirth and renewal of their Spirit" are shutting the Kingdom of Heaven in men's faces. God's grace is His "unmerited favor and spiritual blessing," which means that we didn't earn it, but man sometimes inflicts additional rules outside of what Jesus requires for salvation. Read your Bible, please, because one thing that I have learned in life is that it is the one reliable source.

In Hebrews 12: 18–21 (Amp), the Israelites faced a material mountain that was ablaze with fire. It was a terrifying and phenomenal sight. Even Moses was terrified and aghast with fear. We have not come to such a material, terrifying sight. Verses 22–24 state, "But rather, you have approached Mount Zion, even to the city of the living God, the heavenly Jerusalem, and to countless multitudes of angels in festal gathering, and to the church (assembly) of the First-born who are registered [as citizens] in heaven, and to the Judge Who is God of all, and to the spirits of the righteous [the redeemed in heaven] who have been made perfect; and to Jesus, the Mediator—Go-between, Agent—of a new covenant, and to the sprinkled blood which speaks [of mercy,] a better and nobler and more gracious message than the blood of Abel [which cried out for vengeance]. So see to it that you do not reject Him or refuse to listen to and heed Him Who is speaking [to you now]."

We should be united, carrying each other's burdens and standing strong as one with, and as, the body of Christ, His church. Build up your faith; exercise it like an athlete exercises his muscles. Faith is our spiritual muscle. Know who you are in Christ: a precious child of God redeemed by the blood of Jesus and filled with the Holy Spirit. Forgive others, or God won't forgive you (Matt. 6:15, Amp). Work on these things and help others. Many people are cold and indifferent and simply don't want to get involved. Please have heart and care about your fellow man.

Accept all who come to the Lord and treat them like brothers and sisters, with love. God accepted me and you. Remember that "believeth" means committing to, trusting, and relying on, and that means to Jesus, not to a doctrine of man. It means you really have Jesus in your heart and that you personally know it. The people you see or pass by every day know it too by the light within you. Seek peace among God's family. If someone happily tells you he or she has been born again, don't start waving doctrinal issues at him or her over whether he or she has received this gift, or been baptized that way. I have seen new Christians set back severely by the self-righteous who really *are* shutting Heaven's doors in people's faces. Let that saved person rejoice; smile and rejoice with them. For those who disagree, Paul says in Philippians 3:9 (Amp), "And that I may [actually] be found and known as in Him, not having any (self-achieved) righteousness that can be called my own, based on my obedience to the Law's demands—ritualistic uprightness and [supposed] right standing with God thus acquired—but possessing that [genuine righteousness] which comes through faith in Christ, the Anointed One, the [truly] right standing with God, which comes from God by (saving) faith."

Whatever happened to old-time preachers who preached the way of the cross to Heaven, and of hellfire and damnation at the other end of the spectrum? Those things haven't changed, and we need to realize that obedience and respect have not become obsolete. People used to behave, and train their children to behave, much better than they do now; hell was a serious concern then. What a pampered lot we have become. Sadly, millions will pay an eternal price. There's still hope, but somebody has to care whether we really are a civilized nation any more or not. Or is it politically incorrect to mention that there are grave consequences?

Many modern people feel that preaching about hell is outdated. Hell is still there just like Heaven is still there, and people should be aware of it instead of turning away from a distasteful subject. Ignoring it doesn't remove it. Allow the knowledge of it to help you make good and wise choices.

Sometimes we act like spoiled children who just want things without necessarily giving anything back or expecting any negative consequences. Jesus paid a high price to give us the hope of, and the way to, Heaven. It is the only way that we can avoid hell, and folks need to know about it and what its cost was. By telling us to go and tell the Gospel, Jesus is expecting us to share His love for us and our way of escape with excitement over what we have received, and to share the gift of salvation with the lost. We shouldn't act like children who get up on Christmas morning and see all those gifts that their mom and dad worked hard to provide, with no thought whatsoever of the cost. Children don't understand the cost and show little concern for it. However, the one who paid knows that Santa Claus doesn't really bring all those presents; somebody had to pay for them. I once heard a young mother say that when she determined in her heart to tell her children who the real gift giver is, it was such a relief. She said that she had strongly disliked giving the credit to an old stranger with soot on his clothes. To those who understand, they are aware that all good and perfect gifts are from God. Our children need to know that too. If we are Christian people, we should not act according to the ungrateful and self-centered ways of the world. If the light of Christ is within you, share it and let it shine so that others can also be blessed. He provides gifts, and we as the recipients should acknowledge Him.

My son Greg plays bass guitar on the praise team at our church. He works in construction and is manly, handsome, bright, and kindhearted. In the nursing home where my mother is, it is not at all unusual to see him approach the elderly folks with tenderness and a kind word. Because joy shows through his spirit, they are all so glad when they see him coming down the hall toward their wheelchairs. On more than one occasion, I have seen him crouch down to talk, pat their arms, or bow his head in prayer with one of them. He never brags about his efforts to witness, and he is simply acting out the nature of Jesus that has been placed in his heart. As a matter of fact, I recently heard him tell a story that had happened twenty years ago, and he only told me then because he was reminded of it by the conversation we were having. To me it is an example of letting your little light shine, and truly caring about our fellowman.

Greg, on the job, and always smiling

He said that a friend had come to him to ask his advice about a relationship that he was in, with the notion of moving in with someone prior to marriage. Greg does not have the kind of nature that condemns others, and he is always creative in his responses so that the burden of the responsibility of the decision lies squarely on the one asking. Greg told him that during his latter teens, he had been trying to stop the habit of using marijuana. During that time he had a dream about the exact same subject. He dreamed that he had made it through a few days without the drug when someone came along with the temptation to share one with him. At first he said no, that he was trying to quit. But as Satan does, the tempter continued until Greg said, "Well, okay—just this one more time." During the time that he was smoking it, he heard a thunderous sound in the sky and looked up. He was amazed by the beautiful, magnificent colors of blues and pinks that suddenly revealed an opening, and there stood Jesus on a cloud—coming back to get his children. Greg dropped to his knees in shame and began begging for forgiveness, having been caught in the act. Then he stood, reaching both arms up toward Jesus with his head bowed and his eyes closed—like a child waiting for Jesus to take him too and forgive him again, as He had done so many times before. After a few minutes he opened his eyes and looked up. The sky had returned to normal, and he truly had been left behind. It was a horrifying dream. The friend that he was sharing that story with was stunned at the thought and said, "Man, that's some heavy stuff. I'm not living with anybody until I get married." Greg said, "Good." It was also a wonderful blessing when I heard this next testimony from my amazing son—especially amazing because he is a Christian, is joyful and kind, is willing to spread the Gospel, and feels a responsibility toward others.

Greg and Tylan Grace realized that the man they saw just ahead of them on the street was most likely a homeless person, because not only was he dressed in camouflage clothing, but he was pushing a wheelbarrow also painted in camouflage, laden with what seemed to be his personal possessions. Greg stopped his truck beside the man and said, "Hey, man, what's going on?" That started a conversation, and it continued in small talk for a few minutes. Then Greg asked him if he happened to have a Bible in his wheelbarrow. The man said, "Maybe somewhere, but I really don't read it because I don't understand it, and besides I'm not sure that I believe in God." Greg smiled at him and said in a pleasant way, "Well, this God that you are not so sure you believe in just told me to stop and give you twenty dollars."

Trust God's Word. Live right, do right, think right, and act right. It's amazing what freedom and blessings that will bring. It's our job—not a "nine to five" with payment of money. It's a spiritually motivated, highly desired, and highly pursued mission for the noblest cause of all: doing our part toward the salvation of man and toward the furtherance of the Gospel of our Lord Jesus. Because you're included in the offer of the greatest gift ever known to man, don't you want to accept it and then help others not end up in hell?

Have you ever led anyone to the Lord? It will bless you beyond belief even though the reason you are doing it is for the other person's blessing. There were many instances in the bookstore ministry when we were allowed the blessing of having someone accept the Lord in our presence. That would be an expected place to witness such an event. As a different example, though, I also led two young employees to the Lord in a Hardee's ladies' room. One was crying her heart out, and the other came in to check on her friend. I dared to offer a word of comfort, and they both ended up accepting Jesus. It is challenging to insert yourself into other people's situations. God did not say it would always be easy, but He did say He would always be with us, and if you don't try then you will never know. Reaching out when you see a need is one of those pebbles you either drop in the pond or not.

Having a hospital waiting-room ministry opened many successful doors. What a life when you dare to get involved in Christ's work. I no longer know how many people I have been involved with in their acceptance of Jesus—and I will never stop trying. On one occasion, Scottie and I had sat down beside a young couple at the Med, in Memphis. I noticed that the young man, who sat beside me, was looking through a book that was filled with vile, witchcraft-type photographs. I casually asked him what he had paid for the magazine. He said two dollars. I said I would give him five dollars for it. He was amazed but agreed. I gave him the money and he gave me the magazine. Then I calmly tore it down the middle. He was shocked and asked why

I had paid him for it and then tore it up. I responded that I did so because it was filled with demonic material that I knew Jesus would disapprove of, and that I had wanted to be able to discuss Jesus with him. I asked if he understood why Jesus would not like anyone choosing a satanic magazine for their entertainment. He said that he hadn't thought about that at all, and by that point we were in a conversation that was proceeding comfortably. We talked for a while before he decided that he would like to accept Jesus in his heart. His girlfriend began to cry and said that she had wanted him to become saved for a long time. Praise God! It is my desire to remain sensitive and aware, and to be alert for the call of spiritual rescue. I am neither aggressive nor impolite. Sometimes the situation provides ways to be creative, and I had given some thought in this situation about how I could open an inoffensive conversation with the young man.

Often I offer a smile and a kind word. If it is by God's hand that I have ventured in, then it will go His way. If not, no harm done. It did not come easy at first; feelings such as unworthiness or timidity bombarded me. But I was presenting God's Word and way, not mine, and I had His strength to call on, not only mine to depend on. We learn by doing, and it does get more comfortable, but even from the very beginning, when I was more timid, it had been a blessing that cannot be compared to any other. Pray about it and then set your timidity to a less sensitive level.

On another occasion I happened to see a very old cultic book in an antique shop. I took it to the desk, enjoying a pleasant conversation with the clerk, and purchased the book. The book wasn't her property to dispose of, and I certainly didn't expect that a note to the owner would prompt him or her to destroy a potential sale. After purchasing it I asked the clerk where her trash basket was, tore the book to make it unsalable, and continued to chat. The clerk did ask why I did that, and I simply told her that because I loved Jesus, I did not want that book to ever become an influence in someone's life. Yes, we do this type of thing knowing that most people will be puzzled by our behavior, but that's just testimony time. Go ahead and be a brave heart, and stay alert for the next opportunity. It's always to be done with sensitivity, in kindness and in love, but it is a job, so stay on it!

This is the encouragement and the love that I have for you. There is nothing better, finer, nobler, or more rewarding than fulfilling your true purpose in this life. Don't hold onto the world (the worldly environment apart from God), because it's totally under Satan's influence and power. See it for what it is. Get going on God's soul-saving cause and do some good by helping people to be reconciled to God, through Jesus, before it's too late—and there will never be a "too late" with worse consequences than this "too late." If you aren't active in some form of effort toward the Kingdom of God, and if you really are born again, where's the love? This is not spoken from a critical spirit—it is just the need to remind people of the truth, the glory, and the Kingdom of God. The fields are white for harvest; let the love loose and be extremely blessed.

I know that my redeemer lives (Job 19:25). Travel the high road with the one who can save the whole world. People need to hear the truth about Him and His Word; they desperately need hope. You can start right from home with family, friends, and neighbors. The truth will set them free, and hope will give them joy. Together truth and hope will provide them with a new life and a new attitude. So do it for love, do it for others, and do it for you. Do it for Heaven's sake.

If you are willing to be used, God will show you your personal way of duty and service. The call on your life begins when you confront the needs of others. Don't say, "All I can do is pray." That makes prayer sound less significant and like a last resort, when it is anything but that! It should always be the first resort. Prayer pulls the power of God down for people's needs. Sincere prayer accomplishes much and is a great and wonderful help. When you are confronted by the needs of others, start by responding to them with God's will in mind instead of your personal convenience or ability. Don't let the devil put the idea into your mind that you don't have time to pray, or that you don't feel comfortable praying out loud. Defeat him at every turn and just go for it. It's the sincerity and the doing that brings results. Remember the nearly forgotten, old-time scripture in Matthew 7:12 about "doing unto others as you would have them do unto you"? Let's make it popular again. It's such a small sacrifice from us to achieve so very much.

Please receive this in the spirit in which it is written. Through the Holy Ghost, I am sent with a message to remind us all that Satan, in his terrible insidious way, has slowly been ACLU-ing, "educating," and politically correcting us out of Christianity, and we have neither established nor held our ground. It is time for Christians to take a stand.

I've been told that if you put a frog in a pan of water on the stove and then raise the temperature very slowly over a long period of time, it will actually allow itself to cook to death. We are called the children of God, and we shouldn't let ourselves be lulled into being cooked. We too have been adjusting to the heat from hell being turned up slowly. We're allowing our people and our country to perish from a lack of godly knowledge. Women are not supposed to marry women; likewise the men (Rom.1). Neither are babies supposed to be murdered. This is not political—it's biblical. These two statements are taken from God's infallible Word and are not based on my opinion. The only reason that these two violations are mentioned are because we call ourselves Christians, then vote against the Word of God, making the violations "lawful". It can't be both ways. When conservative commentators say they don't care what other people do regarding some personal behavioral choices, even though they personally believe that these things are wrong, it doesn't really sound like they *really* care about Christianity. *Really* caring people would take a stand for the Gospel, for the love and sacrifice of Christ, and for the love we are to show toward the lost. If I say that I don't care what you do, then I sound like I don't care about your fate, and I most sincerely do.

With love of God (and country) as the imperative, let's work on this together. Take this seriously, consider it sincerely, and love God all the more for it. If you want to be a soldier in God's army, then take the shield of faith and put on the breastplate of righteousness. The armor prepares us for battle. Prayer is the battlefield, and God's Word is the mighty weapon we are to use for all the saints, and against Satan and all his evil forces (Eph. 6:10–20).

"He who gives this warning and affirms and testifies to these things, says, Yes—it is true. [Surely] I am coming quickly—swiftly, speedily, Amen—so let it be! Yes, come, Lord Jesus! The grace (blessing and favor) of the Lord Jesus Christ, the Messiah be with all the saints—God's holy people [those set apart for God, to be, as it were, exclusively His]" (Rev. 22:20–21). Amen—so let it be!

The greatness and majesty of God accentuate the smallness of man. His magnificence magnifies our insignificance. Size and significance are two different things. We are small and also significant to Him because He died for us, but who are we that He should want us?

> **Only a love that is divine would cause Him to reach this far down to put His arms around such a desperately lost people and then lift us up to His kind heart. He gives us our full stature by the infilling presence of Christ within our hearts and souls. I am so very glad that I am allowed to be included, aren't you?**

This chapter ends as it began. Praise Him in the high places; praise Him in the low places. Stay really close to Him. Trust Him always with everything. You'll be in very good hands.

God bless you and I love you,
Dian

Chapter Five

So What Is Your Testimony, Anyway?

Faith is an active spiritual force. Like gravity it pushes and presses against whatever obstacle is in its path until it achieves its goal. It goes over, under, around, and through whatever is in its way. God has given us the right to use faith as a tool to get the job done. It's one of the most powerful witnesses we have to give for our God—to believe Him for a particular thing and then be able to tell about it. He is mighty and worthy to be praised. Faith is a weapon of our warfare against the devil. Whatever he does to cause negative circumstances, take up the Word against him and put those circumstances under your feet. Use it for whatever you need with courage and strength; never mind what the world thinks. My faith has been used for things most people would never even think of using faith on, like praying for an oven that had stopped working to work again for just one more hour, in a crisis—and it did. Faith is for big things and little things.

About three years ago, I was told that I had a blockage in a cerebral artery; it was too deep to do anything about. My doctor gave me the initial diagnosis, and then later was blessed to give me a clear report. In the meantime I was sent from him to a neurological doctor in Memphis who confirmed the diagnosis. At first I was frightened, and then I got serious about using the Word of God against the enemy. Fear was cast down, and the Word was sent forth in faith, believing. Approximately a year later, after another scan was performed, I was told that the blockage no longer existed. That is just one in hundreds of times that God has freed me through His Word, with faith being used to activate His power.

I once heard Ken Copeland tell a story about a time when he had not been a Christian for very long, and he found himself going to God, still again, over a small matter. I suppose that he thought that he might be asking too often for things that might seem trivial to God, and so he said to God, "Lord, I'm sorry that I keep coming to you with every little thing," and the Lord replied to him in his spirit, "Son, it's *all* little to me." Now that's the right perspective! God likes to help us and to have us come to Him, to depend on Him and to put faith into action. Learn to trust Him with everything. Don't limit yourself and don't limit God. If you do, you may be boxed in to your situation by your own doing. He's given you the way and the right to be free, so accept His offer.

We can't demonstrate the power of God if we do things the world's way—those ways are failing miserably without God as a guide. Put some spiritual muscle behind your faith; apply pressure, push, and don't give up. Don't let up, don't give in, and for the Gospel's sake, don't quit. Remember the armor He told us to put on in Ephesians chapter six? Well, He said lift up *over all, the covering shield of faith,* upon which you can quench the fiery darts (or flaming missiles) of the evil one. It doesn't say lay low, duck, or flail your arms about. So where are our shields? Why are we so exposed when the enemy attacks? God loves it when we use our faith; that's what He gave it to us for.

As born-again Christians who are God's people and are set apart for his purposes, we are not to be viewed as downtrodden, woe-is-me, mealymouthed, shrinking violets who are somewhat insecure, somewhat strange, and lacking in higher learning. I am here to tell you that my higher learning is from the most high God, the highest of all and the God of Heaven and earth. He is my keeper; my life is in His hands, and I will continue to pursue

His bright and shining way versus the evil way of the world. He offers me great love, direction, encouragement, and courage to be an overcomer—the object of which is to be a good example for the sake of the Gospel and to have the kind of testimony that convinces folks that there are great benefits to being a Christian, such as joy, health, success, and a good attitude. Psalm 103 talks about some of our benefits, and Deuteronomy 28:1–14 describes good benefits in the covenant God made with Abraham. Our lives may really be the only Bible some folks ever read, so I want my life to reflect the goodness and mercy that rains down on us from Heaven. If we live in fear—fear of lack, fear of harm, fear of ailments or disease—we are placing ourselves smack in Satan's path, and in all likelihood we will be trounced. Living in fear is the opposite of living in faith; it's like flipping a coin: heads or tails, which will it be? Did you ever think that if we are living with negative expectations, we are putting more faith in the devil than we are in God? Think about it.

Picture a group of kindergartners playing outside when a sudden downpour begins. They scatter and cry in panic—but give them an umbrella, and they still play. They lift it over their heads with more sense than we lift the shield of faith over our heads in the storms of life. If staying dry in a storm makes us look smarter than getting soaked, then it gives a pretty powerful picture of whether we put our trust in our God. Shame on you if you don't use your cover to prove your God's truth and power. However, if the light of Christ shines out from under your umbrella of faith because you weathered the storm, then you have a positive testimony. Just in the area of healing alone, I have personally witnessed numerous good testimonies. God has also caused His favor to give advantages in business transactions, to bring joy into a gloomy day, and to do things too many to mention. It is amazing what can be achieved by faith alone, without you having to do anything more than just trust God. I believe that He enjoys responding to faith because it pleases Him when we do trust Him. The Bible does say that without faith, it is impossible to please Him (Heb. 11:6). That's motivation enough!

Ask yourself these questions: Do your coworkers, neighbors, friends, or family view you as a person who is noticeably blessed and who is pleased to give God the glory? Do they see you as someone whom they view as being tested with difficult trials and never having success, or do they see you as someone who is just hanging on and just getting by? How do you answer when someone asks, "How are you today?" or "What's up?" Do you answer by beginning with your medical or financial situation and then continue in a downward spiral about "poor me"? Do you claim, "Please consider me a faith-filled Christian—or maybe a suffering saint, but I'm going through this for God's glory." Please tell me about how a failure in your faith and testimony can bring glory to God. It surely will not make someone want to become a Christian, and it can be discouraging to one who already is. He's glorified when He's lifted up and believed and then given the credit for a positive outcome, if you spoke faith-filled words and obtained a good report. Faith activates God the way electricity activates your television, and He's waiting to be activated by us. Answer by saying that He's working in your behalf; give people a positive, faith-filled testimony when they ask how you are.

So where in the world is your light or your positive testimony? Is it under that ole bushel? Come on, let it out. Use your weapon of warfare against the devil and get out your shield of faith. Prove that there's power in the name of Jesus; get happy, be joyful, and tell of the good things of God. Get excited and show it because it's your job. Have a revival all by yourself, and then with your family and friends and with me. Don't wait for another preacher; you probably have a great one already, and maybe a church family also. Even if you don't, you do have a Bible and a personal relationship with an awesome God. Find some brothers and sisters so that you can have fellowship and love. Get your enthusiasm back, and remember that the object of your heart and mouth, and our job as Christians, is not to grumble and complain, but to patiently await our solution with good hope, enduring the wait with trust in God and knowing that we will come out of it being more Christ-like for having kept our faith strong. Remember that God did not keep Daniel out of the lion's den, or Joseph from being sold into slavery, or David out of the battle against Goliath. However, He was with them, and they came out as historic men of God. It is also worth noting that the trials didn't kill them!

When a person gives you permission to use a little bit of his or her time, which he or she does when he or she greets you with a question about your well-being, go for it. Bless them – don't depress them. Don't glorify what Satan is trying to do; you know who to glorify. Act like you really believe that God is good and that He saves and is real; state that miracles really do happen, that mountains can be moved, and that there's joy in the Lord. Proclaim that if God is for us, who can be against us? He does give us the desires of our heart, so for goodness sake and for the Gospel's sake, say something good that reflects positively on God. One of my friend's constant responses was, "Where I go, Satan trembles," and her joy and confidence always brought joy to those around her. We could say, "All is well with my soul," or "Jesus is alive and well," or "People with the Word are armed and dangerous to the devil," or "Thank God for my next breath, and for the fact that Heaven is my home."

Think of it like this. Everywhere you go you have the opportunity to plant either seeds or weeds; you can sow to grow because there's fertile soil everywhere. One preacher said that God is so great and so good that our eagerness to tell should make us leave the house every day like our shirttail is on fire. How's that for the right kind of enthusiasm? Now, go spread the good news and have and enjoy life to the full, till it overflows. He is the good shepherd, and He did lay down His life for us (John 10:10, Amp). Give our mighty God praise with your heart, with your words, and with your life—how about if we lined up our attitude with our gratitude? That has the potential to be powerful, don't you think? Go forth and conquer, and receive this in love, and in Jesus's name, Amen.

God bless you, and I love you,
Dian

Chapter Six

Living on the Edge

Have you ever thought about the fact that reacting with anger and rage toward someone could be an act (either briefly or long-term) of not forgiving—and do you know what God says about not forgiving? Did you know that there is no word "unforgiveness" in the dictionary? That is quite remarkable, don't you think? It's like a state of being that is prohibited to exist. Perhaps you choose to justify your behavior by saying that you are only human—well, that's the sort of thing Jesus is hoping to avoid from our behavior. "For if you forgive people their trespasses—that is, their reckless and willful sins, leaving them, letting them go and giving up resentment—your heavenly Father will also forgive you. But if you do not forgive others their trespasses, their reckless and willful sins, leaving them, letting them go and giving up resentment—neither will your Father forgive you your trespasses" (Matt. 6:14–15, Amp). That is a lot to think about. We have to forgive others if we want God to forgive us.

There are subtle ways of not forgiving that don't show but are quietly seething. Then there are times when you resurrect the "old man" (Col. 3:8–9) when somebody gets in your face, and you push *him* in his or her face, screaming—well, you can see the downside of that idea. Lashing out in anger is not okay with God, and neither is demonstrating out-of-control meanness, cursing, screaming, or even quietly letting the poison do its work through sulking, pouting, and the like. You are acting like the devil, and you have then placed yourself in another kingdom's domain, and surely you don't want to do that. Think to yourself, "Who is ruler of me now?" You have just allowed the devil to make you feel offended, wronged by another, and caught up in unforgiving behavior, either within that moment of time or for an ongoing period of time. You never know what spiritually good thing you may miss when not being obedient to God. Kind words instead of hurtful words could have been spoken in blessing and love, and the outcome could have been sweet.

When we are born again in Christ, Colossians 3 says our renewed self should now put off anger, wrath, malice, blasphemy, and filthy language. "Do not lie to one another, since you have put off the old man with his deeds and have put on the new man who is renewed in knowledge according to the image of Him who created him" (Col. 3:9–10, KJV). We have put off the old, and must now put on the new. It is our new nature.

Second Corinthians 5:17 (KJV) says, "Therefore if any man be in Christ, he is a new creature; old things are passed away; behold, all things are become new." Ephesians 4:23 (KJV) states, "And be renewed in the spirit of your mind."

There are people who seem to have forgotten that their "old sinful man" (man meaning a member of mankind, whether male or female) was buried when the new, Christ-like man came forth at the time of their conversion. When they accepted Jesus Christ as the Lord and King of their life, they agreed to live by a different standard—His—operating through the principle of love. Do you look around and wonder whether there are any people who have placed themselves under the authority of God and His way of doing things—regardless of whether it's convenient or inconvenient?

> **Where there is a kingdom, a king rules. The king has dominion over the people, and the people abide under subjection to him. The old man of our past nature does not subject himself to the authority of God, so when you allow that "old man" to dominate your life, you are completely ignoring your King, and you are definitely living on the edge.**

I don't know for sure, but you may even be out there without God.

God put a particular story in Numbers 22 to show how destructive anger can be. Balaam was a prophet riding along on his little donkey. God sent the Angel of the Lord as an adversary against him because he was not in good standing with God at that particular time. Balaam's donkey saw the Angel of the Lord, though it should have been Balaam who saw him. The donkey turned aside out of the way, and Balaam struck her. It happened again, and Balaam was so angry that he wanted to kill the donkey. At the third appearance of the Angel of the Lord, the donkey had lain down on the ground. "And the Lord opened the mouth of the donkey, and she said to Balaam, What have I done to you that you should strike me these three times? Balaam told her that he wished he could kill her because he was provoked. The donkey reminded Balaam that he had ridden her all his life and that she had never done anything to him before. Then Balaam saw the Angel of the Lord, bowed his head and fell flat on his face" (28–31). This is an example of (1) God speaking through a donkey to get the attention of a man of God who was very distracted by worldly things, (2) anger causing someone to not even know that God was right in front of him or her (3) anger causing a person to do harm to the innocent, and (4) the likelihood of falling in the presence of the Lord, *if one recognizes that He is there—beyond the distractions.*

Stop and think before you react. Introduce the "new man" to your old ways and let him do away with them altogether. Our new man (ruled by and subject to God) has new ways for us that are far superior to the old. Forgive first, and the offense won't occur, because there would be nothing to be offended about. There would be no reason to act out any of the rest of a bad scene that the devil would have you to do as his puppet, like a selfish, spoiled child. If you do what he wants, the devil gloats because he was able to entice you to go against the God of glory and Father of Heaven. If you discipline yourself to stay in a forgiving mode, these guilt-causing reactions will cease. You can refuse to be offended, believe it or not; it is actually quite enjoyable to see yourself handling situations that would have offended or irritated you before, but now your new response is in a calm, sweet way instead. Offensive remarks by people who still operate through their old man cause those people to be puzzled when you handle the offenses with a gentle spirit. They cannot fail to notice that you have just been a good witness for Jesus through your behavior. It is possible to hold a different opinion without inflicting emotional injury or pain, without arguing, and without sinning. Seek and keep peace, love, and order in your heart.

Realize that children might be expected to respond in anger, but when they do we correct them, or at least we should. However if you are an adult, obey Jesus; He is the father in our case, and we are His children. We usually think that we have no one in charge of us, but we do, whether we submit to it or not. He is still King. Not acknowledging Him doesn't keep Him from seeing us or our lack of faith or lack of love.

Pretend you are two years old. You know what a car is and that it takes you to Grandma's house, so cars are good. Your knowledge is limited, of course, and you have no idea of a car's weight, force, or deadly power. But you're told cars can hurt, so don't play in the street. If your daddy (God, in our case) says not to play in the street, then obey him because he really does know best. If you don't respectfully obey the one with knowledge, wisdom, and authority, then you are placing yourself in mortal danger. No one can simply explain all of the whys and wherefores to a two-year-old. We are the two-year-olds operating under the protection and guidance of our father, God. His vast domain of knowledge, wisdom, and authority is His Kingdom, and we have the tremendous privilege and honor of being His children. However, we must actively choose to obey, because He doesn't force the rules upon us. If you decide to play in the street, that's your choice, but in my heart I feel a serious need to warn against that, because it will separate you from God.

Now, the object of this hope that I have in you is that you will see and apply God's direction in all areas of your life. The area of not forgiving, though, causes much stress and pain, and it can be destructive for all participants. People don't seem to take it very seriously as a sin. It is one that we should see as a very grave situation. It is a sin that could lead to your spiritual death, and its force can torture the heart of those against whom it is set.

The next four paragraphs are taken from the scriptures of explanation found in the *Amplified Bible* in the Book of Matthew. Chapters 6 and 7 will be used as the authority of God on how we are to react to offenses. May it be believed and received as it is explained in the book of "how to live this life and to make it into the next, more glorious one."

1. If you forgive people their violations against you, whether large or small, by letting it go and giving up resentment, your heavenly Father will forgive you. If you do not forgive, neither will your Father forgive you your violations against Him. Your treasures are stored up in Heaven, and your goal in this life is to end up in Heaven. That is worth far more than reacting to anxiety and worry, and in a manner forbidden by God. Where is your faith? Don't you believe that God really has everything under control? Remember, "Without faith it is impossible to please God." We

simply need to go along with Him, and keep seeking His Kingdom as the one great desire of our heart, not getting bogged down and tangled up in the extremely trivial things of life (especially as compared to God's purpose).

2. Don't judge and criticize and condemn others, so that you won't be judged and criticized and condemned yourself and condemned along the same lines that you used to dish it out to them (from some displays of anger that I have seen, that could be a really scary thing—some might even call them savage). Besides, why are you criticizing someone else so, when you have some negatives of your own? Concentrate on making yourself a better person instead of being hard on others, and use this opportunity to discipline yourself in the area of forgiveness for starters, which is vitally important—important enough for disobedience to keep you out of Heaven, and you probably don't want to accept that trade-off.

3. If you want people to do good to you and for you, then do good to them and for them. Remember, this is the Golden Rule, and never doubt that God really is watching. Disobedience, and doing your own thing, doesn't exactly cause blessings to rain down upon your head. The way into Heaven, which surely you desire to obtain and take seriously, is through a narrow gate that is contracted by pressure. The pressure may make it difficult at times for us to do the right thing and to go against what our bodies and minds want to do, but keep your focus on God and what is right, and see to it that you do it. If you don't, then you can take a wide, easy path to hell. There will not be all that many people who stand up to the pressure of the narrow gate, as Heaven is a Pearl of Great Price, and

doesn't come cheaply. Loving, forgiving, and giving are very important areas to God. There will be people who come to you looking like fantastic Christians on the outside, but are evil inside. If you want to be able to tell, and avoid the evildoers, then a helpful suggestion is to think of it like this: Do people pick grapes from thorn bushes or figs from thistles? Of course not. In other words, every healthy, sound tree bears good fruit—worthy of admiration; but sickly, decaying, worthless trees bear worthless fruit. Every tree that doesn't bear good fruit is cut down and cast into the fire. Therefore, you will know them by their fruits, or their beliefs and behavior, combined. If they talk of Heaven but live by the outlaw rules of hell, then you will be able to recognize whether they are your brothers and sisters in Christ. Likewise, other Christians can recognize the spirit under which you operate. Our conversations reveal more than what we're thinking. We never judge anyone's soul, but we are allowed to recognize right from wrong behavior, and to respond appropriately. For one example, it is very uncomfortable to be around an unforgiving person, especially one who is very touchy, easily offended, and quick to anger. The presence of impressionable little children, who should be being taught the language of love, makes it even more of an offense before God.

4. Jesus says that not everyone who calls themselves a Christian will enter the gates of Heaven, unless they do as God says. Many people will call him "Lord" and try to make claims about their own righteousness, but He will say to them openly, "Depart from Me, you who act wickedly—disregarding my commands. If you regard my words and act upon them, obeying them like a sensible, wise person, you will be like

> a person who has built his house upon a rock, and
> when the rains came and the winds blew, his house
> stood because it was built upon the rock. However,
> everyone who hears these words of Mine and does not
> do them will be like a stupid, foolish person who has
> built his house upon the sand—and the rain fell, and
> the floods came, and the winds blew and beat against
> that house, and it fell, and great and complete was the
> fall of it."

Regarding those two chapter explanations, Jesus knows and requires our hearts. He does not accept an outward show of religion, no matter how grand it may be. His will is that we sincerely believe in Jesus. This involves an extremely personal, powerful submission of your heart. If we take Him seriously, we "hear and do," not just hear. We want to be like Him and to live as holy as we can, striving for a more excellent way. Be very aware that much teaching and preaching has gone forth that has wrongly convinced people that a trip to the altar (just to try to avoid hell, when they don't really have a sincere heart) is all it takes. Thousands of people are living under this sadly false impression. It's this simple: if you don't mind others sinning, or you have a casual attitude toward sinning; if dirty or violent movies don't bother you, or filthy talk doesn't, especially from yourself; or if you really aren't comfortable talking about Jesus, or having fellowship with other Christians, then you need to reexamine your situation and hold it up for honest scrutiny. You may be playing in the street, and a car just turned the corner.

You can't believe simply because of head knowledge that Jesus exists, either. The Bible says that even the demons believe and tremble (Jas. 2:19, Amp). You have to understand that an emotional moment and a religious profession of belief will not get you to Heaven; this is frivolous. If you are truly accepting the doctrine of God, then you will want to show humility, grace, and love—you will want to clean up your act. Take this ever so seriously, please. God loves you. Forgive others and ask God to forgive you. What I have just told you is true. Learn more regarding His rules about forgiveness of others if you consider yourself a Christian while not behaving in the way He says. The greatest danger here is in fooling yourself. Don't run unchecked with a worldly heart and an attitude that encourages you in vanity and false hope. Realize where your real hope comes from; where you want to live in eternity (the next step out and away from this life); and how much more wonderful, gracious, peaceful, and good the real presence of God is, and then enjoy the true meaning of blessed assurance. Assurance is when you know without a doubt that you are right with God and that you are definitely going to Heaven. Father God is reaching out His hand of tender mercy and grace to you; you will never regret it—take it now. Take it sweetly and be blessed for the rest of your life, in this life and on into the next. See you there, and I am really looking forward to it. God bless you, and I love you in Jesus's name.

Love,
Dian

Chapter Seven

When You Know for Sure What God's Will Is

Are "Thou shalt not steal" or "Thou shalt not kill" commands from God, and if so, do we need to inquire of Him as to what His will is on these subjects? Emphatic statements declare His will. Would you ever pray, "Let Robin Hood not steal, if it be thy will," as though you think it could possibly be His will for Robin Hood to steal? Would you ever say, "Let Jim Jones not kill, if it be thy will," as though you think it could possibly be His will for Jim Jones to kill? Yes, this is belaboring the subject, but the point is very important. There are personal questions in life, such as whether to make a big move for a new job, or whether or not to marry, or what college to attend. It is a wise and desirable thing to submit your personal decisions before God for personal guidance and wisdom, to want Him included in the details of your life, and to seek His will for specifics that have not been addressed or declared as settled for all to see and go by, in His book of life. He is a personal God and is always available to us for individual counsel.

It is also wise and desirable to accept what He does say as an absolute when He tells us His will on something. Then, our adding "if it be thy will" implies that He might reconsider and rethink what He has already declared. There is neither sense nor reason in that. If He says, "Thou shalt not kill or steal," His will is clear. He wants us to take His Word as final on the subject. He wants us to believe in His goodness, compassion, wisdom, and authority. These are infinite nonreversible qualities, and what He says on any given subject in the book of life is "yea and amen." If God has declared His force of spiritual law on a subject, but things take a different direction in the natural world, then it has gone according to man and his choices or lack of will—not God's. When we prayed, and the person we prayed for had great faith, and God did not answer according to our hope, we must not question it. There are far too many possibilities relating to man that could have interfered, but this I do know: it is never a case of man being righteous and God not being righteous. I have heard people say that a person had died from an illness after being prayed for, so if believers prayed and the person who died was a Christian, then why didn't God heal him or her? We simply cannot give people all the credit for getting everything right, thus leaving God as the questionable party. That is backward in logic.

In the Lord's Prayer, Jesus says, "Thy Kingdom come, thy will be done." That is not a question about whether it should be done or whether it will be done. It is a statement of agreement that His Kingdom will definitely be ushered in, because God has willed it to be and has said so. While we wait, we are to trust and obey. Follow His Word, which is His will. Don't rely on your summary of the situation. We aren't smart enough to second-guess Him. Just do as He says with patience, hope, fervent prayer, and faith, knowing that we are doing our best when we follow our all-knowing God's instructions from one situation to the next. He will consummate His rule and see His Kingdom ushered in, all in His own time.

If I am sick and suffering before it is my time to go, I pray that I am among brothers and sisters who will pray for me with gusto, not tagging on "if it be thy will." In *Merriam-Webster's Dictionary,* the word "if" means "on condition that." Pray like you believe God's Word without conditions. God didn't put any conditions on His Word regarding His part of the bargain, so why should we?

Pray like you believe the great I AM. "Saying, If you will diligently hearken to the voice of the Lord your God, and will do what is right in His sight, and will listen to and obey His commandments and keep all His statutes, I will put none of the diseases upon you which I brought upon the Egyptians; for I am the God that healeth thee" (Ex.15:26, Amp). My hopes will be dashed if you don't believe it and pray it with all your heart. The stripes from that whip lashed His body, causing unendurable suffering and pain in order for us to be able to claim that "by His stripes we were healed" (1 Pet. 2:24; Is. 53:5), and I refuse to go along with a "maybe" on that kind of sacrifice. I am totally grateful and I believe. He's the promisor; we're the promisee. He provides the promise; we provide the faith—the littleness of our faith won't get it, and throwing in those untimely ifs won't either. When you pray, give it all you've got. That's what God wants us to do. Every time you should believe your very best. Don't try to provide a loophole for failure; make a divine connection and don't let anything shake you loose, not even "if." I know with settled assurance that His will is for healing, and settled assurance doesn't settle for anything less.

The reason I am so certain is because God says so in many scriptures. In Psalm 91, He makes it perfectly clear that divine healing is offered as a benefit to people who have made the Most High their refuge and dwelling place. So where is your dwelling place-what is your spiritual address? Let's live in the shadow of the Most High, where safety lies. If God's Word says it, then it's better than money in the bank. Psalm 103:2–5 (Amp) says, "Bless—affectionately, gratefully praise—the Lord, O my soul and forget not [one of] all His benefits, Who forgives [every one of] all your iniquities, Who heals [each of] all your diseases; Who redeems your life from the pit and corruption; Who beautifies, dignifies and crowns you with loving-kindness and tender mercies; Who satisfied your mouth [your necessity and desire at your personal age] with good; so that your youth, renewed, is like the eagle's [strong, overcoming soaring]!" If that is not a scripture to live by, then I don't know what is.

The Word is alive and powerful (Heb. 4:12, Amp), and when you use it on a situation in faith, it goes forth with a power and life of its own (self-fulfilling power—Is. 61:11, Amp), accomplishing that which it is sent forth to do. It is like having the power of God come down. He watches over His Word to perform it (Jer. 1:12, Amp), and He won't let us misdirect it against someone. In Matthew chapter 4 (Amp), when Jesus was in the wilderness and the devil tried to tempt Him, every answer Jesus gave began with "it is written," and then He quoted a scripture. Not once did He say, "If it's okay with God." God says, "I would (meaning my will is) that you prosper and be in health, even as your soul prospers" (3 John 1:2, Amp). We can't convince people to receive healing by confusing them. In the New Testament, in every single incident where someone came to Jesus for healing, He healed them. Not once did He turn anyone down, or say, "If it be thy will." He knew the Father's will and was working in perfect sync with Him, not only to convince the people of God's truthfulness and power, but to do exactly what the Spirit of God directed. He hasn't changed; He is the same yesterday, today, and forever and He never changes (Heb. 13:8, Amp). He said, "I will," which is His will, and He healed them all. Receive it and rejoice—believe it completely, pray it sincerely, and leave the details to God. He is more concerned with your obedience than with your personal prayer victories. Remember that "without faith it is impossible to please God" (Heb. 11:6, KJV). They're His victories whichever way it goes, because He doesn't make mistakes. There are always reasons and mysteries of God that are unknown to us. Read Matthew chapters 8–9 (in an *Amplified Bible*, if possible) and study those examples of healing. If the situation takes a different turn from your hope, don't let your ego be involved. In other words, He knows how the overall plan fits together; we don't. We could have had a shortage of faith when we prayed for a sick person (and that is not blaming or accusing, just speculating on possibilities), or the person we were praying for could be asking God to just let him or her come on home to Heaven. There are many human variables involved that could produce different results other than what we were personally hoping for, but the point is that healing can be accomplished through faith and prayer, and we should put our hope and faith on healing each time as though it was the first, and as though it will succeed. If the person isn't healed, don't give up. I have actually heard people say that they did give up on believing in healing when they prayed for someone and the person didn't get healed. That is music to Satan's ears. Stand by God, and He will stand by you. The next person you pray for could receive divine healing. He's looking out for all His children with a gigantic plan woven together by His mighty hand. Just follow the rules that you understand, have faith, pray, and leave the rest to Him. Accept any final result as though God Himself had been in charge. He always was and always is.

Our obedience is definitely to our advantage in achieving His will in our lives. If we are obedient to Him, then He remains the focus, with us telling others about what God did, not what we did. There are thousands of promises from God in His Word, and they each say what His will is on many different subjects. We should let people see the results of what a walk with God can achieve, by following His Word and the leading of His spirit. The world around us should be able to see and want to have access to Him because of what they see in us. Have power in your prayers based on faith in God, believing and acting on His Word. Doing so achieves results that can be seen, and therein lie our living testimonies. If we pray all the time and nothing ever happens, won't folks wonder why we spend all that time praying? That won't convince them of much for the Gospel's sake. Sincerity as a Christian and in trusting Jesus is the only way to have an appealing testimony about God's love and power. It is His will for us to go and tell the Gospel. How can we be effective in that if we haven't followed what and how He says to learn and do, so that our enthusiasm shows through? It is His will to return for a glorious church. If there is nothing extraordinary going on in your spiritual life, then pray for the Holy Spirit and power.

Let's help make it happen by doing what He says. Believe, pray, receive, and give God the glory. It is His will that we present His goodness shining forth from results received through following His instructions, teachings, and practices.

Sometimes people ask about His will regarding death. It is comforting for people to be assured by the Word concerning the attitude that we should have when a Christian goes on to Heaven. For one thing, God doesn't look at death from a human perspective. We started out in Heaven before life was breathed into us at our conception. We became human beings to live on the earth, and hopefully by the end of human life, we will have actually received His special training in becoming a person of Christian faith and character. "But we are citizens of the state (commonwealth, homeland) which is in heaven, and from it also we earnestly and patiently await [the coming of] the Lord Jesus Christ, the Messiah [as] Savior" (Phil. 3:20, Amp).

We should rejoice when a saint goes home to Heaven, because 2 Timothy 1:10 (Amp) tells us that Christ has annulled death and made it of no effect, and that He brought life and immortality—that is, immunity from eternal death. "Now also we would not have you ignorant, brethren, about those who fall asleep [in death], that you may not grieve [for them] as the rest do who have no hope [beyond the grave]. For since we believe that Jesus died and rose again, even so God will also bring with Him through Jesus those who have fallen asleep [in death] … Therefore comfort and encourage one another with these words" (1 Thes. 4:13–14, 18, Amp). The opposite of the word grieve is rejoice. Paul says in Philippians 1:21 (Amp), "For me, to live is Christ—His life in me; and to die is gain—[the gain of the glory of eternity]." Physical death is not life ended; it is to graduate out of this world's system into eternal life in Heaven. Revelation14:13 (Amp) says, "Then I heard further, [perceiving the distinct words of] a voice from Heaven saying, Write this: Blessed—happy, to be envied—are the dead from now on who die in the Lord: Yes, blessed—happy, to be envied indeed—says the Spirit, [in] that they may rest from their labors, for the works (deeds) do follow (attend, accompany) them!" Psalm 116:15 (Amp) states, "Precious (important and no light matter) in the sight of the Lord is the death of His saints— His loving ones." We need to have respect and reverence for Jesus in siding with how He does things, and we should be imitators of Christ. However, most all of the time there is a heaviness of grief, and it is often used as catalyst to question God's goodness and even one's faith. This is our human nature.

The devil has gained a lot of control regarding the cemetery. The burial ceremony described in Genesis 10:50 (Amp) says that "they mourned with a great lamentation and extreme demonstrations of sorrow [according to Egyptian custom]." We are not Egyptians; Egypt has always been an enemy of Israel. It is so important to remember that our spirit has priority over our body and that our spirit never dies. "So then, we are always full of good and hopeful and confident courage; we know that while we are at home in the body we are abroad from the home with the Lord [that is promised us]. For we walk by faith [that is, we regulate our lives and conduct ourselves by our conviction or belief respecting man's relationship to God and divine things, with trust and holy fervor; thus we walk] not by sight or appearance. [Yes] we have confident and hopeful courage, and are well-pleased rather to be away from home out of the body and be at home with the Lord. Therefore, whether we are at home [on earth away from Him] or away from home [and with Him], we are constantly ambitious and strive earnestly to be well-pleasing to Him" (2 Cor. 5:6–9, Amp). That's worth (physically) dying for, and what a day of rejoicing that will be. Be willing to put your life in His hands, before and after physical death. After all, at this very moment He keeps gravity active so that we don't all go drifting off into space, so He has all the power needed to control our whereabouts. We need to humble ourselves before Him and be assured and glad to trust Him with our lives and our decisions. It will never be the case where we are right and He is wrong.

He is the most high, all-powerful, great and everlasting God, and He has unconquerable strength and gives assurance of everlasting, all-sufficient provision for us. That is His will; He is our provider. Now, think about Jesus: He is here to make things right for us. When we call on His name, we are calling on all of the power and authority that created the universe. He is not just the baby in the manger, or a meek and mild Jesus. He certainly is all of those things, praise God, and He is to be honored for every aspect of His being. However, He is now the risen Savior, as described in Revelation 1. Picture this person the next time you call on Jesus to accomplish what He wills, according to whatever you are praying for. It will raise your faith and trust level. He is here for us, with all that He is. He gives us information like this for us to use and through which to have success. Angels are also included in your having success. Luke 4:10–11 (Amp) says, "For it is written, 'He will give His angels charge of you, to guard and watch over you closely and carefully; and on their hands they will bear you up, lest you strike your foot against a stone.'"

The following description of Jesus is based on the *Amplified Bible* version of Revelation 1:9–18. The picture of His person is the image important to this thought. The emphasis is mine.

> I (John) was in the Spirit—rapt in His power—and I heard behind me *a great voice like the calling of a war trumpet.* Then I turned to see whose was the voice that was speaking to me, and I saw seven golden lampstands, and in the midst of the lampstands *One like a Son of man, clothed with a robe which reached to His feet and with a wide band of gold around his chest. His head and His hair were white like white wool, as white as snow, and His eyes flashed like a flame of fire. His feet glowed like bright burnished bronze as it is refined in a furnace, and His voice was like the sound of many waters (like thundering waves of the ocean!) In His right hand He held seven stars, and from His mouth there came forth a sharp two-edged sword,*

and His face was like the sun shining in full power at midday. When I saw Him I fell at His feet as if dead. But He laid His right hand on me and said, "Do not be afraid. I am the First and the Last and the Ever-living One—I am living in the eternity of eternities. I died, but see I am alive for evermore; and I possess the keys of Death and Hades (the realm of the dead)."

This is the power and the glory of the risen Christ. If you will picture Him when you pray, your expectations and faith will rise to new heights. He is the Holy One, the God whose Word I am asking you to stand strong on. He is the one who means it the way He says it, and that is His will on any given subject. It is written for our good and for us to obey—not to question, just obey. Glorify Him, honor Him, and believe Him every time about everything He says. How can you not believe something that has been willed to us through the last written will and testament of the God who rides on the wings of glory? This is a picture of my God, the one who answers our prayers in advance, because He has already told us in His book what to expect and what He will do—what He has willed to us based only on our condition to believe, trust, and obey. I believe our mighty God; don't you?

God bless you all (how I love God's family and mine, and that includes you). Amen.

Love,
Dian

Chapter Eight

Forgiven or Forbidden

For many years my heart has wanted to raise this question. Are we recognizable as Christians to those who know us, or do we just claim to be because we are churchgoers? Do we follow the Golden Rule and really do unto others as we would have them do unto us, or is that just our church face? Matthew 7 says that we should be easily recognized by what our lives produce. My serious concern has been that many (though certainly not all) preachers have been too enthusiastic toward gaining their number of converts. They have represented salvation to be as simple as a verbal commitment. They encourage people to come to the altar, which is good, but when people are in an emotional moment and are scared, they sometimes go for a misunderstood reason: they are just trying to escape hell. It is not necessarily because they want or intend to change their lifestyle, but because they think that if they vocalize a plan of salvation, followed by water baptism, they'll be saved by grace and can continue to live the same way they had been living all along. Many well-meaning TV preachers (not all) offer a verbal shortcut to salvation, when they fail to explain the whole truth to folks. There's not nearly enough emphasis put on the word "repent" and the serious meaning of it. To repent means to be sorry, to turn and go the other way (which would be away from sin and back toward God). It means to turn away from immoral deeds and to dedicate oneself to the amendment of one's life as a lifetime commitment. Neither is there enough emphasis put on the word "believe." These are key issues on whether one is forgiven or forbidden in Heaven. To believe for salvation is to spiritually accept Christ.

To be saved means that if you were drowning and someone saved you, then you would have been delivered away from a death experience and back into one of life. You would never forget that experience, would you? To be spiritually saved is to be delivered from a death experience—eternal death—a death which means that one will be alienated from God forever, along with all the pain and wailing miseries that accompany it. If you agree to receive God's way of life into your heart as a new way to live, and if you also believe in your heart (not just your head) that Jesus is the Son of God who died on the cross for our sins, was buried, and then rose from the dead as a sacrifice for us, then tell Him so. Tell Him that you are very grateful for the price that Jesus paid for our salvation and that you fully intend to behave His way instead of the world's way from that point on. Make it clear to yourself that you mean to live by this decision and sincerely intend to change your old way of life through the indwelling presence of the Holy Spirit of God helping you. That help should be welcomed by you and not resisted. When you feel that you understand the commitment that you are agreeing to make, then take the solemn pledge of believing, receiving, and accepting the offer from God of salvation. That death penalty will be erased, and you will receive eternal life. No one will expect perfection from you. You will then be welcomed into the fellowship and presence of God, with all the blessings and joy that accompany that choice.

When I came face to face with the *reality* of God, I saw that there was an extreme contrast between a worldly life and a godly life. I was made to question whether I was forgiven by the Father or forbidden from glory. What had darkened my understanding before was lack of knowledge. If you are living with His presence in your life daily, you have awareness daily. He offers comfort, gives you answers, guides your conscience, and generally is your very best friend. In no way is He intrusive, unless you consider it intrusive regarding your conscience. Letting your conscience be your guide is actually a great recommendation if you know right from wrong. It is guidance provided by His precious love. Spiritual children of God cannot be born of human, natural descent, but only by the spirit of God, the Holy Spirit dwelling within us. Our willing desire that He guides our lives is the life-changing offer that we make to God, when we accept His life saving invitation.

In John 3:3 (Amp), Jesus said that if we are not born again, we can never get into the Kingdom of God. I know that "Just as I Am" is how we go to the altar, but we are not supposed to leave the altar the same way we arrived. When we leave we need to change our tune to "I Will Follow Jesus" or "I Surrender All." At least there should be some leaving song to encourage a new approach to joyful transformation. We are not supposed to be going back to our seat just as we were—but many do. This is not like a fairy tale where the frog (an unbeliever) gets turned into the prince (son of a king), just because someone kisses him (a preacher says so). I use a silly example because there are some who treat the Gospel lightly and do not take going to the altar seriously. It is an enormous mistake to treat salvation lightly and to not be dead serious when you approach His altar. You do not experience spiritual rebirth when you do that. God is calling us to a life of purity and holiness (which means, according to the *Amplified Bible*, "separation from sin, with simple trust and hearty obedience," Ps. 93:5), and to spreading the Gospel, and it is a very serious choice that we need to make in order to save our spiritual, eternal life. Taking tradition for granted will be an eternal mistake. Thinking that you have escaped damnation by making a show of going to the altar is an eternal mistake. This is serious, and we need to wake up to the truth. If we are not truly born again when Jesus completes the final gathering up of His people, the true believers, then those remaining will be left to burn. You *must* be born-again. I honestly thought that being saved and being born again were two different conditions. They are one and the same.

"But the day of the Lord will come as a thief, and then the heavens will vanish (pass away) with a thunderous crash, and the [material] elements [of the universe] will be dissolved with fire, and the earth and the works that are upon it will be burned up" (2 Pet. 3:10, Amp).

I recently heard on TV that now only about 64 percent of Americans claim to be Christians. Ten years ago it was more like 90 percent. What exactly does a claim to be Christian imply? In *Merriam-Webster's Dictionary* the first meaning shown for the word "Christian" is an adherent of Christianity.

> **In John 3:3 we see the beginning of a new life in Christ, or, of one who adheres enough to qualify as a Christian as stated by Jesus (Amp). "Jesus answered him, I assure you, most solemnly I tell you, that unless a person is born again (anew, from above), he cannot ever see—know, be acquainted with [and experience]—the Kingdom of God." Those are the words of Jesus on the first step to becoming an adherent in the biblical meaning of the word.**

In Acts chapters 1 and 2, we are told about the day of Pentecost and the great outpouring of the Holy Spirit on those who were assembled there. In Acts 2:21 (Amp) Peter says, "And it shall be that whosoever shall call upon the name of the Lord—that is, invoking, adoring and worshipping the Lord (Christ)—shall be saved."

At that time, before the Holy Spirit descended upon them, there were many devout men, believers in God, people who had been baptized by John and who were followers of Jesus. In Acts 11:11, Peter tells how the Holy Spirit instructed him to accompany some men "without [the least] hesitation or misgivings, or discrimination," which would be an example of following the leading of the Holy Spirit, which is expected of people who are Christians. In verse 16 Peter says, "Then I recalled the declaration of the Lord, how He said, John indeed baptized with water, but you shall be baptized with—placed in, introduced into—the Holy Spirit." Verse 21 says, "And the presence of the Lord was with them with power, so that a great number [learned] to believe—to adhere to and trust in and rely on the Lord—and turned and surrendered themselves to Him." Then, after all of these things had occurred, it says at the end of verse 26, "and in Antioch the disciples were first called Christians." Christianity does not mean just wanting to appear respectable by going to church on Sunday. According to what we read in John 3:3, the words that say one must be born again from above means that there is no such thing as a "non-born-again" Christian. Many Christians consider themselves Christians without a true born-again experience. They are simply acting religious and think they are saved because of their religious tradition. The words in John 3:3 came from Jesus, not me. The word "Ichabod" in the Bible means that "the glory has departed." Many churches are in that category, and many professing Christians choose that type of church based on their ideas of respectability and solemn behavior. That behavior has evolved from man-made ideas. Modern churches expect that they should seek the ministers who have the most degrees, display the best choirs, have the best programs, and generally appeal to the most people according to the world's standards. But what about the power and the glory? In the words of John in Matthew 3:11 (KJV), "I indeed baptize you with water unto repentance: but he that cometh after me is mightier than I, whose shoes I am not worthy to bear: he shall baptize you with the Holy Ghost, and with fire." For clarity, the Wuest New Testament explains that last term as "He (Jesus) himself will baptize you *in the sphere of and by means of the Holy Spirit and fire.*" *The Spirit-Filled Life Bible* says in the note beneath this same scripture, "As John's baptism placed the individual in the medium of water, so the *baptism of Jesus places the Christian in the Spirit, identifying him as bound over totally to the Lord.* Fire either purifies or destroys. Hence, salvation in Jesus will be purifying for the true Jews who accept Him as Messiah and destructive for those who reject Him." (True Jews would include us too, as having been grafted into the Tribe of Judah through accepting Jesus as Messiah.) This paragraph is a very good explanation of Acts 2:38 also.

However many claim to be Christians, they should be using the above standard in determining their true status. If we really had even 64 percent of our population as born-again Christians, actually thinking and behaving as Christians, then how in the world could our country be in such a state of affairs? The real question here is about our true relationship with Christ—and whether we really even have one or not, except in times of crisis. I feel the need to ask, though: Where are all the Christians? Statistics do show that Christianity is on the decline. According to ReligiousTolerance.org, prior to 1990, Christianity in the United States was at about 87 percent. Then many Americans disaffiliated themselves from Christianity. By 2008, the number was 76 percent, with the decline continuing.

If those statistics were acquired by counting according to the truly high standard of the Bible, instead of man's opinion of himself, the *true* percentage may have barely even gotten off the ground. Obviously if we were explaining Christianity accurately, it wouldn't be declining. We need to live at a higher level of personal behavior and to receive prayer results by genuine faith. God's Word should be being used in our prayers, with us rejoicing over all that is working well, not mumbling about all that is wrong and pitiful. If our responses were based on our personal positive relationships with God, then our report of God's grace and love would speak forth in joyful testimony. The Gospel, which we are supposed to be telling about, is not another offer of the world's ways of negativity and failure. The people who aren't living for God certainly don't want more of what they already have.

Instead of offering folks (as a comparison) a lovely package that is empty—we should be offering them a "hope" diamond, made by God and being worth thousands of God's promises. Our speech should reflect the ways of God through our positive attitude and spiritual success, in our prayers, our health, and our joy.

Matthew 7:21–23 (Wuest Expanded Translation) states, "Not everyone who keeps on saying to me, Lord, Lord, shall enter into the Kingdom of heaven, *but he who keeps on doing that which my Father who is in Heaven has determined shall be done.* Many shall say to me in that day, Lord, Lord, did we not in your Name prophesy, and in your Name cast out demons and in your Name perform many miracles which demonstrated the power of God? And then I will declare in a public announcement to them, *I never came to know you experientially.* Be going away from me, you who are working the lawlessness" (emphasis added). "Experientially" means having experiences with. *Merriam-Webster's Dictionary* defines "lawlessness" as "not being regulated by, nor based on law, not restrained, nor controlled by law." In the case of the scripture, it refers to God's law.

> **We can believe in God or Jesus intellectually, without having a renewed heart or a desire to really be regulated, restrained, or controlled by Him. I know that because the Bible says "even the demons believe, and tremble" (Jas. 2:19, Amp), and we know that they aren't going to Heaven! We can combine intellectual knowledge with being water baptized, but it still won't get us to Heaven. Without the desire for a life-changing experience through an encounter with the Holy Spirit of the living God, all we get is misled and wet.**

There is no wonder that so many people are falling away from organized religion. Many people haven't gotten hold of the real thing yet, and counterfeits don't survive the test. We must be willing to have our behavior regulated, restrained, and controlled by His Word, and dedication seems to sidetrack many. Remember, perfection is not required—just sincere desire.

For you to see for yourself, please have patience and give serious consideration to some chosen scriptures that give very specific warning signs. They are from the Book of 1 John, chapters 3–5 (Amp). The Books of John are very near the end of the Bible, near Revelation. The Book of Revelation reveals how God will destroy all of the forces of evil in all its forms. The following scriptures are seriously important, and so please take them to heart and be blessed. They are words written to us by God's own instructions.

> (1 John 3:4–6, 10) Every one who commits (practices) sin is guilty of lawlessness; for (that is what) sin is, lawlessness (the breaking, violating of God's law by transgression or neglect; being unrestrained and unregulated by His commands and His will). (5) You know that He appeared in visible form and became Man to take away (upon Himself) sins, and in Him there is no sin— essentially and forever. (6) No one who abides in Him—who lives and remains in communion with and in obedience to Him, (deliberately and knowingly) habitually commits (practices) sin. No one who habitually sins has either seen or known Him—or has had an experimental acquaintance with Him.... (10) By this it is made clear who take their nature from God and are His children, and who take their nature from the devil and are his children; no one who does not practice righteousness—who does not conform to God's will in purpose, thought and action—is of God; neither is anyone who does not love his brother (his fellow believer in Christ).

(1 John 4:15, 17, 20–21) Any one who confesses (acknowledges, owns) that Jesus is the Son of God, God abides (lives, makes His home) in him, and he abides (lives, makes his home) in God.... (17) In this (union and communion with Him) love is brought to completion and attains perfection with us, that we may have confidence for the day of judgment—with assurance and boldness to face Him—because as He is, so are we in this world.... (20) If anyone says, I love God, and (detests, abominates) hates his brother (in Christ), he is a liar; for he who does not love his brother whom he has seen, cannot love God Whom he has not seen. (21) And this command (charge, order, and injunction) we have from Him, that he who loves God shall love his brother (believer) also.

(1 John 5:1–5, 19–21) Every one who believes—adheres to, trusts in, and relies (on the fact) that Jesus is the Christ, the Messiah, is a born-again child of God; and every one who loves the Father also loves the one born of Him—His offspring. (2) By this we come to know (recognize and understand) that we love the children of God; when we love God and obey His commands—orders, charges; when we keep His ordinances and are mindful of His precepts and His teaching. (3) For the (true) love of God is this, that we do His commands—keep His ordinances and are mindful of His precepts and teaching. And these orders of His are not irksome—burdensome, oppressive or grievous. (4) For whatever is born of God is victorious over the world; and this is the victory that conquers the world, even our faith.

(5) Who is it that is victorious over (that conquers) the world but he who believes that Jesus is the Son of God—who adheres to, trusts in and relies (on that fact).... (19) We know (positively) that we are of God, and the whole world (around us) is under the power of the evil one. (20) And we (have seen and) know (positively) that the Son of God has (actually) come to this world and has given us understanding and insight progressively to perceive (recognize) and come to know better and more clearly Him Who is true; and we are in Him Who is true, in His Son Jesus Christ, the Messiah. This is the true God and Life eternal. (21) Little children, keep yourselves from idols— false gods (from anything and everything that would occupy the place in your heart due to God, from any sort of substitute for Him that would take first place in your life).

The holiness that we should feel by welcoming Jesus into our lives as a permanent, full-time companion should last for the rest of our lives. It will be based on His purity, not ours, and it should inspire us to separate ourselves from things we may have been doing that are dishonorable to God or in spending time with others who are behaving inappropriately. Something is definitely different about you after you turn your heart over to God. You feel it and you know it. So, if within the few days after your claim to salvation you were back to your old self again, then you should think seriously about whether it was emotional only, or emotional and spiritual—and lasting—and whether you are a better Christian today than you were then. God accepts us at any level so long as it is sincere, but trying to improve should be a continuing desire, and so should loving Him and wanting to know Him better—not trying to play hide-and-seek; just seek, and you shall find!

There was a time in my own life when I was not sure that I was saved, even though I thought I was a Christian. In all the years that I did attend church off and on, I had no impression of anyone really stressing the point of true salvation *being tied to your behavior,* other than the big, most evident sins. No one had ever told me that without faith it would be impossible to please God. My goodness, that in itself is huge! Mostly it was "once saved, always saved," and that forms a false impression when people aren't really saved to begin with but think they are because they went down to the altar and then later were water baptized. During the questionable years of my life, I went about my business from crisis to crisis. When bad things happened, which were quite often, I would cry and pray, huddled in a corner or on my face in the floor. God always helped me, the crisis would pass, and I would go right back to not giving God much thought through my days and nights—until I needed Him again. Actually, I guess I thought of Him as way off somewhere, running the universe. I never recall being taught about a close, personal, constant relationship with Him. Sometimes I would look longingly out a window, often living a long way from home, because in my marriage to Jay we never lived anywhere near where we had grown up. I would think about life and wonder what would satisfy me and where I could find happiness or peace—maybe a different husband, more money, or some kind of different life altogether. Sad to say, if our lives were any different than that of our friends, it wasn't noticeably so, except perhaps for the abuse that I suffered. I still see that mind-set all around me. Because people live so much by worldly standards and see each other living that way, they tend to think it's the norm and think that if they changed and set a new standard, others would just view them as misfits, to which they have some sort of aversion even if it means that they might actually be accused of living godly, wholesome lives. Again I ask where all the Christians are.

I was mentally and physically abused for many years by Jay. Finally, the physical abuse pushed me to the limit. In a violent scene of drunken rage, I had been shoved, hit, and cursed. Pictures were yanked from the walls and slammed to the floor; potted plants were knocked over with dirt flying everywhere. Everything was broken and strewn with glass, picture frames, and anything that he could lift that could be destroyed. The force of my head hitting metal-louvered doors had left them bent. After the house was wrecked, he said he was going to kill me. While he fumbled his way down the hall for the gun, I ran from the house barefoot on a freezing night to the local quick stop, crying and pleading for someone to call 911. It was by the grace of God that I escaped that fate—hurt, dirty, embarrassed, cold, scared, and feeling very alone. That night ended that chapter of my life, of living on the outside of the Good Life, where Satan was running the show.

When I was forty-two years old I married a man named Ralph E. Wells, who was the greatest Christian I had ever known. When I look back, sometimes I wonder whether he was the first real Christian I had known, other than my granny. I'm sure there were others who just weren't that obvious. Mostly it seemed that folks lived by religious practices, but the common attitude in that day was of not discussing religion or politics. But both my husband and my granny were always joyful, singing, and in a good mood. They would talk about Jesus or their politics (conservative) with whomever would listen.

He walked by faith like I had never seen or even heard about. He was so delightful and positive all the time, and I began to see living as a Christian in a way that I absolutely had never seen before—in any church, in any town, or in any country. He was the real McCoy and was definitely recognizable as a Christian. He was strong and manly, but when he prayed, tears would flow down his face—not sadly, just touched by the wonder of God. He definitely set me on the right track, not by stern words or a ruling hand, but by his witness as a person, his faith, and maybe most of all, his positive and joyful attitude. His motto was, "If it can't be done, we can do it," and it works when you believe it! He went home to be with the Lord in 1999. What an unbelievable difference between being married to an ungodly man first, then to a born-again, spirit-filled Christian. Even if we disagreed about something, he never raised his voice, and never did he treat me like I was an inferior person. He called me precious and treated me that way. What a difference the Lord makes! I had finally found real love and a real home.

When I first met him, he was an engineer for the Department of Defense, and he also owned a Christian bookstore in Laurel, Maryland. I worked in an office in the same building as his salaried job, and he was a friend of my boss. For about a year he was just "that nice Mr. Wells who owned a Christian bookstore." At that time I was still married to Jay. Around the time that I left Jay, Mr. Wells and I became better acquainted. He had been divorced for eleven years. Now, I know that this sounds too quaint and a bit strange, but because he was eleven years older than me and had quite a high position, I was accustomed to calling him Mr. Wells. As long as we were married, I never called him Ralph, so it would be out of character for me to do so now. The young people in the bookstore, who were usually students who worked part-time, fondly referred to him as Mr. Ralph. As time went on, I came to refer to him also as either Mr. Ralph or Ralph E.

Sometimes in the afternoons we would go to the bookstore and usually stay until 8:00 or 9:00 p.m., because it was his habit and he dearly loved being in that store. I felt somewhat awkward about it at first, because it was bringing me face-to-face with a previously unknown world. It was a tough schedule, but it became such a wonderful, different world that it started to seem interesting and exciting. His way of life was so unique to me. He didn't drink, smoke, curse, or do any of the normal worldly things around us. It was as though he lived within a separate sort of invisible shield, while still being with and around everybody else. He prayed if someone was sick, and they often had a quick recovery. He was kind, not easily intimidated by any means, and he always handled difficult situations with grace and calm, seeming to know that somehow "everything's gonna' be all right", and it always turned out that way. He was wonderfully unique because of his faith and his refusal to compromise his beliefs. What a great and exciting training camp my life with him turned out to be. His dad had been a preacher, and Mr. Ralph could have easily been that as well. He was lacking in no way regarding knowing and quoting scripture, or in praying on-the-spot, spiritual, moving, successful prayers. Every woman should be so blessed.

His witness to me probably kept me out of hell because he taught me about a real relationship with our heavenly Father. In my new life with him, I learned that nearly everything in my first marriage was wrong and that life with a true Christian man was an experience that should be told and available and lived more often. It resembled a knight in shining armor story, and I know for sure that it was a marriage made in Heaven. If both parties wanted to serve God, that could become the normal relationship of marriage for folks now, instead of a wished-for rarity. That is not the way the world lives or views marriage, so I have to ask again, where are all the Christians? The most important point is about the miracle-working achievements, wrought by God through his faith in the God he loved so much. There was a relationship there that would make anyone question their own relationship with God, because others paled beside his. I determined that if Mr. Ralph could have it, I could too, and he assured me that I could. He constantly reminded me that God was no respecter of persons (Acts 10:34, KJV), and what He does for one, He'll do for all. We spent many years in the Christian bookstore ministry. They were the absolute best years of our lives because we took his ministry, his hands to lay on others in sincere prayer, his joy and positive attitude, and his great faith in God with us unashamedly everywhere, and everything we did worked out well. We had success, were invited on TV programs with our book ministry, saw people saved, healed and delivered, enlarged the store, and had a Christian family like no other in the world with our book- and music-loving friends and customers. It was the most exciting, glorious time anybody could ever have, and I will be eternally grateful for having a real walk with God revealed to me in such a precious, powerful way. Perfection is nowhere close as an achievement, but I keep reaching for more.

After a while, we had become actively involved in the store ministry full-time and were no longer employed elsewhere. It was a way of life so completely different from all others. I loved it then, and now I see ever clearer what an awesome life we led, nearly unheard of these days. We usually were there from 9:00 a.m. to 9:00 p.m., six days a week—but it wasn't tiresome like regular work. We had good music playing; people coming in smiling; people praying (not cursing and lying and betraying); people who were joyful and who believed in miracles, which we witnessed regularly; people who would ask us for prayer (and we would ask them); and people who would give us good reports and gladly give God the glory and praise for His goodness and tender mercies. What a life when a whole little community within the walls of that precious bookstore ministry lives, talks, loves, and actually enjoys the Christian way of life. That was the way it was when you went through the doors of that huge, wonderful, beautiful store, New Life Books and Gifts.

I have been involved in owning three businesses since then, and God miraculously put the TV cameras on two of those businesses, too—creating success again, as He does when He is honored, thanked, and included in whatever we undertake in following His will. What a wonder He is. Nothing is mine; it is His, and for His glory. I take nothing for granted, but I totally believe that God is for us and not against us, and that when we do things in faith, He will cause it to unfold in a wonderful way—especially if ministry is a major part and motive of whatever is being done. He has granted according to His promises and His Word, so I am not afraid of new undertakings or adventures when I become convinced that they are His will for me. Hallelujah!

Mr. Ralph and I were not sin free, as a book like this might hope to imply, but we desired to be. All humans are subject to attacks by Satan, and no one is exempt from that, from the beginning of our lives to the end. However, my heart was filled with joy and great expectations, and the reality of a life lived for Christ remained wonderful in spite of human error, whether large or small. This testimony is to glorify God and to happily express the freedom from guilt and fear that we are allowed to rejoice in when we repent and move ahead. He knows our motives, brings us up and out with His grace when we are sincere in asking for forgiveness, and gives us a continual song in our heart. He is the perfect one.

Spending years in the Christian book ministry was the lesson of a lifetime, and I will always cherish it as so special and memorable. In telling you about some of my experiences with the Christian and non-Christian public, I can truly tell you from experience that many who talk the talk don't walk the walk, and God is not fooled even if people are. Once I heard a preacher say that if you know someone who isn't saved, help him. Otherwise, it's like seeing gasoline poured over that person and then lit with a match. It's a disturbing way to express it, but it does present a terrible truth, and it really is our job to confront reality, not ignore it because it's unappealing. If you can help somebody, please do so. Tell people about the Gospel in a way that will get their souls saved, so that their lives are changed and their eternity is secured. It is not a dull, restrictive life—it's wonderful and exciting. How could a person personally know the living, almighty God and not enjoy life? That's just another one of Satan's lies, and it's a whopper! Let's get real and go for the gold—the golden gates of Heaven, that is.

I am not in any way suggesting that you judge anyone else's soul, but the Bible teaches us what is right and wrong, and if someone is consistently behaving in an immoral, inappropriate manner, then we are allowed to judge right from wrong behavior.

Don't convince yourself that you have no business talking about Jesus with someone about whom you are sincerely concerned. If people are really saved, then they will enjoy the opportunity to have a Christian discussion. I long for people to bring up Christian thoughts and ideas to me, to just talk about the Bible, but I would say that that happens mostly on Sunday, at church. It seems very lopsided to me that people want to talk about everything else, and I mean everything and anything, before they want to talk about the Word, or participate in Christian conversation. The bookstore ministry and being surrounded by spirit-filled people spoiled me for life; it has been a sort of dry, old land outside the wonderful years of spiritual excitement and activity of that everyday environment. None of us thought any of us were perfect, but we loved and helped each other, instead of trying to criticize each other with a "holier than thou" attitude. This love walk is about us wanting to stay on the narrow path and being blessed for trying (and saddened in our heart when we fail); it's about loving God and being forgiven when we do stumble.

Many people think of themselves as saved, you know. It isn't at all likely that anyone goes around for very long with the impression that hell awaits them if they don't accept Jesus. Many professing Christians think that they have already done so, because they have been water baptized, without the spiritually born-again experience. If you ask directly whether or not someone is born-again, which I never do, they feel indignant over the question. When I was on the outside looking in, I honestly did not understand the difference between what most folks refer to as being saved, as compared to the biblical explanation of being born again. Talking about Heaven is a gentler, easier introduction into the subject with someone you sense may not have actually been born-again. Because of a person's attitude, negative speech, and low expectations from God, it sometimes seems likely that he or she is not displaying a trust in Him. Satan has folks fooled into thinking that they have to struggle and sweat, to figure everything out on their own, and to be lonely, broke, and sad—all while being engaged in a fight for their life. Baloney! Satan is such a deceiver and liar. How in the world can people choose that kind of life over the gloriously good life with God? We just need to remember who Satan is—the loser—and God is always the victor. Choosing who you want to believe and go with is pretty simple (see Jos. 24:15, KJV), so that's a good start. But it does take grit and determination to stay with it on the harder challenges. Knowing and believing that Jesus is with you is the key.

The part about believing sincerely, better known as faith, is what will help the anchor hold. Believing in Jesus—and that He loves you, and that He will help you if you let Him do it His way—is at the top of the list of how to weather a storm. But it is the kind of believing that means sticking with Him, which shows true commitment (expected for you to follow through on). That only seems hard for a second, but just consider what you can or cannot do, as compared to what all the power in the universe can do, and then go ahead and turn it over to Him. Let Him be the captain of your ship, and then rejoice because He is.

Jesus came to the earth as the son of God. He was part of God, clothed in human flesh so that we could relate to Him, could see Him as a human and how He behaved, as an example to us. His own precious blood was shed as a sacrifice for us, to prove to us how important we are to Him, and He suffered it all for human eyes to behold. Then He arose from the dead after He had taken the keys of hell and death away from the devil (Rev. 1:18).

Have you ever thought that if we believe humans who are born with a sinful nature, then why don't we believe God, who is holy and pure—and that by not believing Him, we are calling Him a liar? Once you do believe Him, you should believe everything He says because it's all holy and pure. After rising from the dead, He ascended into Heaven but told us not to worry, because He was sending the Holy Spirit (Acts 14:26, Amp) to live within us as a personal guide from Him. We could then have Him present with us at all times and in all situations, until Jesus comes back (1 Thes. 4:16, Amp) to get the people who truly believe in Him and are considered His church.

There is an almighty God who created the heavens and the earth. His Holy Spirit lives within me; I have seen miracle after miracle; have joy, health, and peace uncommon to most; and can tell you truthfully that I know Him personally and know He is real and lives. More unbelievable things have happened as blessings to me than I can even remember, and these things continue to happen on a regular basis.

> **What a friend we have in Jesus. Don't minimize the blessings and favor He shows by thinking that if you talk about Jesus, you won't fit in. If you really think about it, who wants to fit in with people who, because of their ignorance of His Word, diminish His holiness and power by finding it politically and socially incorrect? Truthfully, they are to be pitied and prayed for.**

Don't try to intellectualize yourself out of spirituality; you'll lose unimaginable blessings and happiness, and gain nothing more than agreement from other non-followers who are going to live their lives without the love, help, and joy of the Lord. When you go out on a limb with God, you'll find that you definitely won't fall. Some of my personal testimonies are told throughout these chapters to prove what going out on a limb with God can accomplish, from becoming a new person in Christ to land purchases, to fighting city hall, to overcoming death-threatening fear of snakes, and to the hardest of all: being able to conduct my precious son Scottie's small graveside funeral because there was no other acceptable person available that we knew at that time. God can overcome any kind of obstacle in your life through faith in Him, the power of His Word, and the Holy Spirit of the living God. If I could recall them all, I could fill pages in relating the numerous wonders performed in my life because God said He was with me, and I had the courage to believe Him. He has never let me down; in all the ways that He has been with me, I give Him all the glory.

If you do go out on a limb with God, you will know that Jesus and the Holy Spirit are also with you. Some wonder how

Jesus and the Holy Spirit are all part of God, and how there could still be just one God. Well, you know that an apple has a core, the edible part, and the skin. An egg has a shell, the liquid, and a yolk. A man has a spirit, a soul, and a body. A daddy is a father but can also function as a brother and as a friend to another, with all those relationships suiting each particular relationship's needs. It's one apple, one egg, one man, one God. It's not really hard to understand that there are different functions or assignments or different aspects of God's multifaceted Person. We need to respect Him as Father, Son, and Holy Spirit; each is there to be acknowledged and appreciated for whatever part of God is dealing with us at the time. God is our Creator, Jesus is our Savior, and the Holy Spirit is our guide. They are their own, distinct persons, but are the same one God, serving different spiritual functions in our lives. When we pray, we address our prayers to "Father," as Jesus did. In John 14:25–26 (Amp), Jesus was speaking about all He had been teaching during His ministry on earth: "I have told you these things while I am still with you. But the Comforter, (Counselor, Helper, Intercessor, Advocate, Strengthener, Standby), the Holy Spirit, Whom the Father will send in My name [in My place, to represent Me and act on My behalf], He will teach you all things. And He will cause you to recall—will remind you of, bring to your remembrance—everything I have told you." All of the offices He just described referred to the Holy Spirit and some of His functions. Read that list again. Every need we could possibly have is covered by the Holy Spirit of God, who is constantly available and very capable of fulfilling the promises made to us. Jesus said this is what He would do. He did not say He would force it upon us; we must make Him welcome. Jesus follows that by instructing us to have peace, and not to let our hearts be troubled or afraid. We should stop allowing ourselves to be agitated and disturbed, stop permitting ourselves to be fearful and intimidated and cowardly and unsettled, because He is coming back for us, His church (referred to also as His body). If you contemplate, study, and absorb that scripture as a truth from our real God, into your heart, mind, and spirit, you will receive power from on high by allowing the Holy Spirit to come in, and your life will become bigger than life. Seek Him. This is spiritual reality. Matt. 3:16-17 shows God as our Father in Heaven, the Holy Spirit descending as our powerful helper, and Jesus as our way to salvation, being baptized. Three distinct persons/functions of the one Godhead are represented, but are still one God.

Jesus's precious blood was meant as a powerful commitment to us that if we wanted to come to Heaven someday, our sins and wrongdoings would be covered and washed away, so that we could be clean and free from the filth of sin in the world. When we accept His sacrifice, we have something to offer back to Him in our acceptance and appreciation of what He did. We offer to let Him show us the right way to behave and to guide us in how to live to be pleasing to God. He has given us the right to be free from the power of evil, death, and hell, and we have agreed that we want to be free from it all and to do things the good way, which is His way. He gave us the right for the Holy Spirit to live within us to rule our conscience and direct our behavior. He doesn't expect us to know everything right away or to do it alone, or to get everything right all the time. He is a kind, good Father. Having Him in your life doesn't mean that you will never sin again. We want to please Him, so we strive for that which is good, and we feel sorry when we act unbecomingly. He really wants us to love Him enough to do good rather than evil. When we make mistakes, we must ask Him to forgive us. He is faithful and loving, and He most certainly will forgive us, but He also tells us to forgive whatever we have against others, because if we don't forgive others, He won't forgive us. So you see, He does have some rules of goodness for us to follow, and wisdom from His Word recommends the help of the Holy Spirit. It is important to realize that being born again cannot be achieved through natural means. The supernatural has transformed the natural, and the extraordinary replaces the ordinary. We must have His divine power dwelling within us if we are to achieve our purpose as Christians.

When the Bible gives the command of Jesus that we are to "Go, therefore and make disciples of all nations, baptizing them in the name of the Father, and of the Son, and of the Holy Ghost" in Matthew 28:19 (KJV), and then says in Acts 2:38 (KJV) to be baptized "in the name of Jesus," there is a valuable translation that has gone mostly unnoticed. These scriptures *do not* contradict each other. The error in our understanding is in the use of the word "baptize." This is very important. Dr. David H. Stern is a Jewish man who is also a born-again believer in Jesus the Messiah. He lives in Jerusalem and has great knowledge regarding the Jewish language and culture, both present and past. He has translated and written two books in particular that have become immensely valuable in translating the New Testament more accurately from the original language: *Jewish New Testament* and *Jewish New Testament Commentary*. I have condensed the writings to fewer words without changing the meaning. (See page 156 in the JNT and pages 225–226 in the JNTC). Acts 2:38, as explained in these reference books, states that each individual must repent, through which the underlying Hebrew word not only means turning *from* sin, but *back to* God. The command is to absorb completely and accept totally the work, power, authority, and person of Yeshua (Jesus) the Messiah, and you will receive the gift of the Holy Spirit.

Regarding the word "baptism," it means that our spirit (not our physical body) is to be immersed into the character and nature of Jesus—which is a spiritual immersion of our spirit into His Spirit, so that we come forth from that spiritual immersion (having been changed from our natural human nature to having a supernatural born-again one). No physical act can accomplish that; reborn spirits can only come from above. The baptism spoken of in Acts 2:38 refers to a spiritual baptism. In the natural world, a similar situation would occur in the dipping of a white Easter egg into red dye, with the red dye having *permanently altered the nature* of the egg because the egg took on the dye's nature. And so it is when our spirit is baptized into Jesus's supernatural spirit. This is about the change in our character and nature becoming like Jesus, and is not about a physical ritual cleansing through water baptism. Water baptism only *represents* that you are identifying with Christ in His death, and rising again to the newness of life. First Peter 3:21 (Amp) says that water baptism is a *figure* of deliverance. What it saves us from is inward questionings and fears, providing us with a clear conscience of inward cleanness and peace, because you are demonstrating what you believe to be yours through the resurrection of Jesus. It represents that you have been renewed and cleansed. You are willing to commit yourself to Him and to not be ashamed of the Gospel of Jesus Christ.

This symbolic water-baptism is done by the same authority and power of Father, Son and Holy Spirit, that created the universe in Genesis. Chapter 1, verse 26 refers to our Creator, God, saying "Let Us [Father, Son and Holy Spirit] make mankind in Our image, after Our likeness."

The biblical explanation of why these verses *seem to* say different things is because in Matthew 10:5–6 (NKJV), when the twelve disciples were being sent out, "These twelve Jesus sent out and commanded them, saying 'Do not go into the way of the Gentiles, and do not enter a city of the Samaritans. But go rather to the *lost sheep of the house of Israel.*'" The note below the scripture, referencing verses 5–15, explains that "Jesus instructs His disciples concerning the *scope* of their mission, the substance of their message, the works they are to perform, the equipment they are to take, and their procedure. As a microcosm of the church (Luke 12:32), the mission of the twelve *foreshadowed* the ongoing mission of the church, which would extend beyond the house of Israel (Matthew 10:6) to include a global scope (Acts 1:8)."

In Luke 12:32 (NKJV) Jesus says, "Do not fear, little flock, for it is your Father's good pleasure to give you the kingdom."

In Acts 1:8 (NKJV) states, "But you shall receive power when the Holy Spirit has come upon you; and you shall be witnesses to Me in Jerusalem, and in all Judea and Samaria, and to the end of the earth."

In Acts 2:36 (NKJV) we read, "Therefore *let all the house of Israel know assuredly that God has made this Jesus whom you have crucified, both Lord and Christ.*"

Jesus's command in Matthew 28:19 referred to a worldwide scope of the followers of Christ taking His message to all nations and peoples for the hearing and receiving of the Gospel, which is "the message of Christ, the Kingdom of God, and salvation." In Acts 2:28 (NKJV) Peter wanted to convince the Jewish people, the lost sheep of Israel, God's "little flock," that their longed-for Messiah had in fact come, that they had crucified Him, and that they should accept the will of *God*, turn back to Him and repent, accept that *Jesus* truly was the Son of God and was their longed for Messiah, and to consequently be spiritually immersed into Him. All that having taken place, they would then be under the cleansing blood of Jesus and their sins could be forgiven, after which they would receive the gift of the Holy Spirit.

You do not have to memorize the Bible, or be scared that it presents a list of *no*s and *don't*s. It is definitely a list of *yes*es and *do*s. His presence within us gives us righteousness—not of ourselves, but because part of Christ is living within us, and we are carrying around with us, through Him, a part of God. Is that not a privilege of the highest order? Negatives become positives, blessings come upon you, and it's exciting to be a part of the family of our magnificent God. You must realize that people who have this want to keep it, and that having it shows! You want it forever, certainly enough to cooperate with God when He speaks to your heart or stirs your conscience. It becomes something you would die for. You do not want to look for a comfortable place between what you had before and your new life in Christ. You actually prefer the good, wholesome, clean way, and it is a yoke-breaking blessing to have all that old stuff cleared off of you.

When you start feeling that clean satisfaction down in your soul, and start seeing miracles being performed by the power of the almighty God, and find that your faith and your prayers are pulling the power of God down on things that matter to you and your family—believe me, you won't ever want to go back to the old you and to the empty struggles of the past. I have witnessed salvation, peace, success, healings, jobs found, marriages healed, and too many wondrous things to mention. It's all just waiting for a true believer. Now, your Father is a King—and what is the son or daughter of a king called? You are now either a prince or a princess, with rights and privileges of the Kingdom that you will delight in finding out about. Just be very careful that you always stay humble and grateful and honorable toward Him, and don't try to use Him, which is different from trusting, believing, and honoring Him. Be glad that He wants you; He deserves the very best, and He will give you His best always.

If ever a scripture described my love and feelings for God very accurately and adoringly, it is Isaiah 6:3–8 (Amp): "And one cried to another and said, Holy, holy, holy, is the Lord of hosts; the whole earth is full of His glory. And the foundations of the thresholds shook at the voice of him who cried, and the house filled with smoke. Then said I, Woe is me! For I am undone and ruined, because I am a man of unclean lips, and dwell in the midst of a people of unclean lips; for my eyes have seen the King, the Lord of hosts! Then flew one of the seraphim (heavenly beings) to me, having a live coal in his hand which he had taken with tongs from off the altar; and with it he touched my mouth and said, Lo, this has touched your lips; your iniquity and guilt are taken away, and your sin is completely atoned for and forgiven. Also I heard the voice of the Lord, saying, *Whom shall I send, and who will go for Us? Then said I, Here am I; send me.*"

(The note from the *The Spirit Filled Life Bible* says that Isaiah was not physically touched by the tongs, but that verses 6–7 are part of the vision's symbolism. A sinful man in the presence of the holy one is doomed, but God took the initiative to provide atonement and cleansing because Isaiah was contrite.)

The Word of God is absolutely filled with wisdom, hope, instruction, assurance, and the mention of things too wonderful to imagine. It also contains directions as to how to obtain all of this as a blessed hope for all eternity. The Word is only ever meant for our good and to help us, and we can't just act like spoiled children always wanting to do things the way we please, satisfying our desire rather than disciplining our destiny. If we want to grow up spiritually, we need to be done with childish ways, receive the truth from God's own words, and rejoice that we have a way into His holy presence and out of the grip of sin and hell. It is a good and glorious thing to be loved, taught, and received by our magnificent, glorious God.

We may still have some time left to put ourselves in right standing with God, but most Bible-believing folks also believe that the end is drawing near. If you believe that there is a God but don't know much about Him, I encourage you with all my heart to set your mind and heart on finding out what to expect to happen to both believers and nonbelievers. Their fates are very different. One will be horrific, as Revelation 22:12–14, 17–21 (Amp) shows (emphasis added):

> (12) Behold, I am coming soon, and I shall bring My wages and rewards with Me, to repay and render to each one just what his own actions and his own work merit. (13) I am the Alpha and the Omega, the First and the Last (the Before all and at the End of all). (14) Blessed (happy and to be envied) are those who cleanse their garments that they may have the authority and right to (approach) the tree of life and to enter in through the gates to the city.… (17) The (Holy) Spirit and the bride (the church, the true Christians) say, Come! And let him who is listening say, Come! And let every one come who is thirsty (who is painfully conscious of his need of those things by which the soul is refreshed, supported and strengthened); and whoever (earnestly) desires to do it, let him come and take and appropriate (drink) the Water

of Life without cost. (18) I (personally solemnly) warn every one who listens to the statements of the prophecy (the predictions and the consolations and admonitions pertaining to them) in this book; if any one shall add anything to them, God will add and lay upon him the plagues—the afflictions and the calamities—that are recorded and described in this book. (19) And if any one cancels or takes away from the statements of the book of this prophecy—these predictions relating to Christ's Kingdom and its speedy triumph, together with the consolations and admonitions (warnings) pertaining to them—God will cancel and take away from him his share in the tree of life and in the city of holiness (pure and hallowed) which are described and promised in this book. (20) *He Who gives this warning and affirms and testifies to these things* says, Yes,—it is true and (Surely) I am coming quickly—swiftly, speedily. Amen—so let it be! Yes, come, Lord Jesus! (21) The grace (blessing and favor) of the Lord Jesus Christ, the Messiah be with all the saints—God's holy people (those set apart for God, to be, as it were, exclusively His). Amen—so let it be!

Be saved, be sure, be blessed. Allow His righteousness to make your little light shine. I sincerely love you, and God does too.

Love,
Dian

Chapter Nine

Faith Brings Peace

Genesis 28:16 (Amp) states, "And Jacob awoke from his sleep, and he said, surely the Lord is in the place, and I did not know it." In verse 18, he took the stone he had put under his head and set it up for a monument to God, and he poured oil on its top in dedication. In verse 22, he said, "And this stone, which I have set up as a pillar (monument), shall be God's house (a sacred place to me); and of all (the increase of possessions) that You give me I will give the tenth to You."

We had moved to a desolate place on the Tennessee River, in the southwestern part of Tennessee. It was about halfway between Memphis and Nashville but south of them. It had rough, stony ground. We anointed it with oil. God gave us increase, and I tithed on behalf of our family, cheerfully. I had been taught the principles by which to live and trust God, but I did not have any knowledge of these particular scriptures in Genesis 28 at that time. However, the same God that was there for Jacob gave me the same general plan, and I cannot even imagine all of the disasters that would have befallen us if we had been in that situation without those principles of faith and love being firmly established in our hearts. Thank God for His Word. We must learn and live by the Word in good times. If not, it can be tragic when trials come. Anoint your home with oil. Tithe, and trust God.

From wading above my knees in the flowing, beautiful river of life in our busy wonderful Christian bookstore, where everything seemed as near to Heaven as can be on this earth, to moving to a river bank in a remote, dry, and rocky land, with perils all around, these scriptures are a completely accurate picture of how God orchestrated, and we discussed, then followed Him, in going from one extreme to the other. One was protected, safe, and wonderful in our large, blessed ministry-store. The other was an isolated, wooded world where we had purchased fifty-four acres on the Tennessee River, hedged in by unbelievable difficulties, danger, loneliness, and the unknown. If a sensible person asked why we bought such a situation, I could not give a very sensible answer. I knew that Mr. Ralph was having trouble with his memory, but I thought that it was due to stress. Moving home to Tennessee was the most beckoning for retirement, the river was very appealing, and we thought it would be a great adventure. Well, we were certainly right about that! We were so accustomed to living within easy access of everything that we simply assumed what we needed would just be a longer drive for purchases, or perhaps we could just have things delivered. In other words, we were very naïve. Honestly, we were so accustomed to living by faith that we didn't seriously inquire about the availability of drinking water or how to build a road.

By the time we purchased the land for our new home, the Laurel, Maryland, bookstore had been combined with the Lynchburg, Virginia, store for some time. Within two weeks of our decision to buy the land, we had a buyer for the store. That miracle encouraged us toward following our new plan. Such extraordinary things happened as a result of that move. The story and the outcome for so many people, who were affected in a positive way due to events that could only have happened because of that move to Tennessee, could only have been designed by the hand of God. Highlighting portions of the story will give you a picture of one of the most different kinds of existence to emerge from out of modern, normal people's lives. The real answer is that it was God's will, and we followed like two little sheep, simply believing that Psalm 23 was a personal message to us who believed. Verse 6 (Amp) says, " Surely or only goodness, mercy and unfailing love shall follow me all the days of my life; and through the length of days the house of the Lord [and His presence] shall be my dwelling place." Part of the footnote following that verse says "the Lord would anoint His 'sheep' with the Holy Spirit Whom oil symbolizes, to fit them to engage more freely in His service and run in the way He directs, in heavenly fellowship with Him."

Mr. Ralph and I had been married for seven years. I had known for two years that some health issues were causing him mental confusion, but he seemed physically fit and joyful. We fully expected him to be healed. I felt that moving closer to the family that I did have would be helpful, because the situation required me to make responsible decisions on our behalf, and it was a new role for me. There were some relatives in different nearby towns who were successful people, and I knew that they would be kind to me; though I had never been in close relationships with them, we were fond of each other. The experience they had that I sought most was in the case of one great aunt and her daughter, and it was their prayer and spiritual lives. I had been very accustomed to Mr. Ralph's wise headship over our home and business, and frankly, I didn't want the job. However, I was also accustomed to living by faith and not questioning God (whether things were my choice or not). The world calls Alzheimer's incurable. Those weren't words that we were willing to receive, but at the time of our move to Tennessee, we had not yet heard those words of diagnosis. Faith was a way of life for us, and it still is for me. God sees the big picture, though, and the what and why concerning each of us. Where it came from I don't know, but I appreciate the saying that goes, "It's not for me to question why, it's just for me to do or die." I add "trying" to the end of that saying, and I think of it as referring to our faith. We were now in a new land, facing the new path that God had led us onto.

He is with us and causes us to persevere through the toughest of times and hardships. His presence is everywhere; He keeps us safe. The oil used to anoint does represent the Holy Spirit of God. Put it where you abide, or on your car; put it wherever you frequent. Trust God, love Him, get the spirit of fear out of your life, and take on faith instead—and then tithe to prove that you mean it! Our tithing is not because God needs money. For goodness sake, God doesn't need our money; He owns everything already, though He is not materialistic in any sense of the word. We have money as a convenient means of barter, but some people consider their money more valuable than their obedience, and that is where the principle of tithing comes into play. Yes, God does live where streets are paved with gold, but the purity of the gold and the perfection of the other materials of jasper, pearls, rubies, and more are for the glory and amazing beauty of Heaven. Revelation 21:21 says that the pure gold of the streets of Heaven is like transparent glass. Why would there be a monetary value to anything in Heaven? It is a place of purity, altogether spiritual and most divine! However, because we are still on this earth, we must consider our attitude toward money and whether or not we can part with it for use in efforts toward building up the Kingdom of God. We must consider our attitude toward faith in God regarding our being cared for, versus faith in our money. There is a very true, simple formula for achieving the very best for our well-being on this earth, and that is to not allow fear and greed to keep us from tithing. Apparently, for us to part with money for use in the Kingdom is one of our chief stumbling blocks. Recognize it and get past that kind of thinking. This is the Lord God almighty that you are trusting in, and so actually trust Him. If He's in charge of your life and is your business partner, it would be wise to give Him the small share He has spoken of in His Word. Obviously He is looking for your attitude and obedience. Remember: it's all His already and we're just walking through, but

He is with us (Psalm 23), so if we desire the promises, we should follow His instructions. He personally has promised all of us that we will be blessed if we follow our heavenly CEO's financial advice. In 2 Corinthians 9:7 (NKJV) it says, "So let each one give as he purposes in his heart, not grudgingly or of necessity; for God loves a cheerful giver." I am so grateful for the teaching about the tithe that I had learned early in my walk with God. He absolutely will not let you down on this subject if you tithe with the right spirit, and not just with the idea of getting something from Him in return.

Based on faith, our hearts followed God's leading to this new home amid thousands of acres of undeveloped land. The road we had to build from the highway to our new home site, on a cove of the river, was one mile long, through woods and rocky terrain. We had arrived in the fall of 1989. It was the following summer before the road was drivable. The owls we heard hooting just outside our motor home didn't seem so cute when we discovered that they were really coyotes. On more than one occasion we were told that there were panthers too. We thought the local folks were just trying to have their fun with us, until one was actually seen by a family member.

Other houses or cabins were sparsely located, maybe a mile or two down the river or down the highway. It took us three years to build our home to a livable condition. The mile of road was a special challenge. Because of the remote location, everything seemed to become a major project. We proved that folks could still be pioneers in Tennessee.

The bedroom of our motor home had two twin beds, one on each side of the center aisle. One night just after the lights were turned out, we heard what seemed to be something very large climbing up the ladder to the roof. Then it became more terrifying as it moved about on the top. Remember, this was a dark night in the deep woods. It can be hard to think when your mind wants to pass out from fear. Faith, Faith, where are you? The walls seemed really thin at that point. I whispered to Mr. Ralph that if we both screamed and yelled as loudly as we could, and banged on the walls at the same time, maybe we could scare it away. I took his silence for consent but later discovered that he hadn't understood. Anyway, I took a really deep breath, got as much air as I could, and attempted to calm down long enough to try my idea. I whispered "In Jesus's name" and then made the most piercing scream of my lifetime while loudly, desperately banging the wall. After a minute or two of silence, both inside and out, I whispered, "Do you think it's gone?" There was still silence for a minute more before Mr. Ralph replied, "I think it's lying out there on its back somewhere, with all fours legs in the air—and my own skin has tightened up all over my body!" That became one our funniest memories. What a time we had on our pioneer adventure. We never knew who or what our big visitor was, but I imagined him never wanting to climb that hill again.

We certainly confronted many kinds of fear on many occasions. God kept us safe; we only had Him, and He was certainly enough.

> **There was no 911 or a neighbor to call, and no storm shelter. God reminded me that we had "91," though—as in Psalm 91. It is filled with promises about our well-being, and they are yours as well as mine! We were two little humans—one not well, the other not brave or strong—against tremendous elements and dangers.**

There were times when the walls did shake and the mighty winds did blow. We could see the treetops through the skylight of our little camper, under such force that they were nearly parallel to the ground, with noise like a train roaring by. Neither our little camper nor our construction site suffered any damage after two different tornadoes traveled down the river past us and over the top of us, destroying the marina at Clifton, Tennessee, one mile down the river. Our physical inability had nothing to do with

God's power. After our house was completed, another mighty wind blew. I remember standing in a hallway with both hands reached out and pressed against the hall walls, feeling the house shake and tremble, and I never stopping the stream of scriptures coming out of my mouth. It is written, "No weapon formed against us shall prosper" (Is. 54:17). "When the enemy comes in, like a flood the Spirit of the Lord will lift up a standard against him" (Is. 59:19). "If God be for us, who can be against us" (Rom. 8:31). "He makes even our enemies to be at peace with us" (Prov. 16:7). "For God hath not given us a spirit of fear" (2 Tim. 1:7). "The Lord rebuke you!" (Jude 1:9). When I couldn't think of new scriptures, I would just shout the same ones over and over. If you know only one, it's still the Word of God and will defeat Satan. I am an all-for-God believer, and God has kept me safe. Our faith in Him had everything to do with our ability and our survival. We lived because of the power and truthfulness of God and His Word. If worldly attitudes say that we survived by coincidence, then I try not to get too angry when simpletons try to steal God's glory and turn it over to chance or coincidence.

I *know* that God was with us, and I would face the wilderness all over again. Every time fear challenges me, I do my very best to overcome the flesh (the human body apart from the spirit) and to defeat fear with the much more powerful force of faith, energized and activated by the Word. I often wondered on dark nights whether our tiny light could even be seen as a twinkle when looking down from among the stars.

Our land and our dwelling place were anointed with oil, which is an act of faith as well. It has no special qualities of its own, but when placed in faith, it represents the Holy Spirit, His presence, and His protection. We prayed together and individually, in the spirit, as well as with our understanding. We believed; we named our road Covenant Cove Lane. The name originated from our gratitude for the covenant God made with Abraham (Deut. 28), and we as believers claim as ours too. One person who knew very little about the Bible said, "Hmm, Coconut Cove—that's nice." That's actually a reasonable comparison to how the general public fails to receive the available power and attention to detail of God. God did mighty things, and He hasn't stopped. He'll show Himself mighty in your behalf just as quickly in New York City as He did for us in the wilderness. God's children's faith isn't perfect; our Jesus is. He knew our hearts and honored the faith that we had set before Him. He knew our weaknesses and provided us with His strength. When I say set before Him, I do not only mean placed before Him, but also with faith set like having been set in stone!

My life with God has been one of extremes and adventures. The tragedies and hardships have at times been such that I was barely able to survive, but any time when I couldn't feel His presence, I learned in a hurry to seek Him. He was always there with comfort and love. I knew that I could trust His goodwill and love for all of us. He gives us the right to a special kind of life when we decide to really believe. We need to know Him as comforter and strengthener and guide.

In this very remote region of the country, we suffered a culture shock regarding Christianity that was more threatening, disturbing, and hurtful than the natural threats. We would never have dreamed that such a strange attitude from our new community would turn out to be so heartless. Our life before our move there had been a true oasis in the desert, spiritually speaking. We had left behind our large, beautiful, nondenominational Christian bookstore. It was a place of love, praise, ministry, prayer, and miracles. Pastor friends said we had a spirit of excellence regarding that store. We worked there joyfully and had a steady flow of great fellowship with other believers. We loved it with all our hearts, but because Mr. Ralph's health was being challenged, our move to the next chapter of our lives became necessary.

Missing the store and the ministry would be difficult, we knew, but, really we *didn't* know. It's good for Christians to live by faith, because if we had known what a spiritually dry place we were headed for, we would have probably been reluctant to accept that idea as being from God. I was born in Tennessee and live in Tennessee now, and there are some great folks here. This experience happened in an isolated, undeveloped part that surely is unique in its mind-set.

People seemed curious about us but aloof, making it obvious that we weren't one of them. We were actually referred to as a cult. We had unintentionally offended their country pride when we refused the offer of what is commonly called a water witch, which locals thought we had to have in order to determine where to drill a well. By habit, we talked about God's willingness to use His power to show Himself mighty in our behalf. They, by habit, still wanted to use a diviner, which the Bible forbids. We are not to seek knowledge through other means than the Lord, our God. "For these nations, whom you shall dispossess, listen to soothsayers and diviners, but as for you, the Lord your God has not allowed you to do so" (Duet.18:14, Amp). He has afforded us the benefit of divinely appointed, godly sources of information. The abundance in our hearts made us speak faith to a people who had not been exposed to that kind of teaching. There was a heavy spirit of negativity that you could almost feel in the air. Their Christianity was different from ours. The well driller was reported to be a minister of the Gospel. We were too extreme and different, and they just didn't get us—and they really didn't seem to want to. Even though I had lived in that same kind of area as a child, I hadn't realized at the time how slowly change comes to areas that just keep passing their ways from one generation to another, with no one interested in change.

A young man from Liberty University, located in Lynchburg, Virginia, who was selling Bibles during a summer break, was told to stay clear of our house because of our unusual beliefs. Bless him for braving it, because we had a rare and good time of fellowship with him. He had actually been in our store in Lynchburg and knew some folks who we knew. In going from such a spiritually high and happy life where we were loved and respected, to being thought of as practically demonic is quite an unexpected trial! Neighbors did not understand the term "spirit-filled Christians," and they certainly didn't think of themselves that way. We did, and we were very different from them: positive compared to negative; joyful compared to feeling defeated all the time; believing in divine healing and anything else divine that God chose to do compared to accepting any and all woes and illness as being from God. It's pretty much the same list that Christians who are committed to God face with the world every day. This was different and felt more intense because there was only one family of us. The rest of the community was what seemed to be opposed to faith in their religious beliefs.

People who want to disagree with faith-motivated Christians about healing, prosperity, provision, and care from God have difficulty understanding my devotion to God after some of the particular trials that I have had. But that's the point: if we stick with Him, He will stick with us. Their logic seems to be that if faith-filled Christians don't have their prayers answered the way they hope for, then they are either wrong in their expectation, or God has simply let them down. The best way to sum up the most common attitude is, "I never have had anything, and I never will." That is one of the biggest lies of Satan, straight from the pits of hell. It only proves that critics don't really know God, who is always operating for the good of His entire family.

It is my desire to keep Jesus's face constantly before me, spiritually speaking. I want to love and trust God the way He wants me to. Reaching higher is my style. I am determined that however sad and difficult some trials have been or will be, or however weak and ignorant I can be and have been at times, I will continue to trust Him. If I don't, I will fail, because I am definitely not smarter than God. He is my rock, and there is no unrighteousness in Him (Ps. 92:15, Amp). He is always good and always right. I know that when the waves settle, calm waters will reflect His glorious mercy. He is my God, and in Him will I continually trust. Romans 8:28 (Amp) says, "We are assured and know that [God being a partner in their labor], all things work together and are [fitting into a plan] for good to those who love God and are called according to [His] design and purpose." When doors of opportunity have opened for me, I may have tried to peek in and around a bit, but I have followed what I thought to be God's leading. I wouldn't change lives with anybody; God has been so good to me, and I have had a really good, interesting, rewarding life. He will do the same for anyone who will trust Him. Even in spite of the hardships of my marriage to Jay, I had my two precious sons, saw the world, and appreciated the good that was there. God has given me courage and interest along with faith (without which I would have done none of my exploits). Anyone who lives very long will face trials. It's the degree of genuine trust in God's goodness, and His motive being for our good, that keeps us anchored in Him even as the sea of life sometimes billows and rolls.

We had a well drilled without the use of a diviner, and it was a very strong well, but like others in that area it contained sulfur. A system was installed to remove the sulfur, but we still needed a source of normal water because our current source was causing much hardship. Sulfur is very damaging to plumbing and to kitchen and bathroom fixtures. We prayed for our well to be sulfur free, but God had a different idea in mind. I was about to face another challenge beyond illness, wilderness, snakes, storms, condemnation, and isolation.

My husband's and my oldest son's illnesses, followed by their consequent deaths, were definitely the hardest trials of my life. Having moved there was another trial—because until you've been cut off from friends and neighbors to whom you can relate, who comfort you and converse with you and appreciate that you have *some* worth, you cannot imagine how lonely life can be. Try living without love. No, on second thought, don't. Another lesson of life emerged from those times: we can make it without outside support, as long as God is with us. Through our weakness He is made strong. Our survival is proof of His existence. If all that was achieved had been placed in our hands only, we'd still be living in the camper in the woods.

Most of my family thought that I was a religious nut, and they were providing little or no support. When I had first been filled with the Holy Spirit back in Virginia, they said, "You've moved to the country and lost your mind." I understood their concern even though I knew they were wrong, and I held no ill feelings toward them for it. I ask for your prayers, for my life to be a witness to them. Let's get on with God's business and not be hung up on each other's failures, because God isn't. That is another dirty trick of the devil, to try to discredit people over their past. What God cleanses is clean. Please don't inflict even more pain. Live life based on today, not yesterday, so that we can all help folks face tomorrow—with God and His army of saints, who were all made free from sins.

The loss of someone does not in any way express the pain from the loss. My son, Scottie, died from AIDS after we moved to Tennessee. The torment had lasted for three long years before he went to be with the Lord. He was a born-again Christian when he died, and he and I joined forces with God and spent many hours of testimony and ministry in hospital and clinic waiting rooms during that time. Only God really knows how many of our efforts of testimony may have resulted in eternal salvation. Scottie had been living at home with us on the river for most of his last year, where he was usually confined to his bed. He suffered terribly. Test or treatments were sometimes given him in the hospital that were very painful, like the size of the needle pushed between the ribs in his back used to draw accumulated fluid off the lungs, or the tube pushed through the nose and down the throat into the stomach. On one occasion, because cancer had begun to spread throughout his body, they used radiation on a lesion between his teeth and inner cheek. They burned a hole in his cheek that kept him hospitalized for seventeen days; he was given Demerol for pain. Later, near death, they refused to give him the pain medicine for relief because they said that he was now technically considered a drug addict, based on the length of time that they had given him Demerol during that previous stay.

Another time, I waited in the hall of the hospital while a doctor used some sort of laser treatment to try to reattach the retina of his eye. I listened to the zaps over and over and over and knew that it was hurting Scottie. When one is a mother, being restrained by (necessary) boundaries from removing your child from pain can produce anxiety and stress that can end your life if you don't know God very personally. I did not understand, but I had learned to trust God through practice on smaller things, and it gave me the heart toward His goodness that I needed when the need was enormous. Near the end, with Scottie's hair growing back in little sprigs here and there and him being so skinny and frail, he said to me one day that he felt like someone's raggedy doll that they had just tossed away. Pain, pain, pain. Unless you've seen your child suffer so, you cannot imagine what I suffered. He was so very sick. God was still there for us, and during the final six weeks, the pain miraculously ceased. My gratitude will last forever for that touch from the Master's hand. Thank you, Father.

The generally harsh attitude of the people in our new hometown showed that they would not have been forgiving toward our family situation. I conducted Scottie's graveside service because, at that time, we knew of no clergyman in that area who would do so without prejudice. I could not bear the thought of a hypocrite speaking over my precious son. We were very aware that there was fear, prejudice, and hypocrisy everywhere around us. There was rumored to be a KKK meeting held regularly within a few miles of our home, and based on general conversation that we had heard, it was obvious that burning a house to the ground wouldn't seem too extreme, if done so for one of the KKK's unholy causes. We were Christians and needed love, prayer, and support more than ever. We were not only left to face our difficulties alone, but their behavior and prejudice added to our suffering.

My husband had been diagnosed with Alzheimer's about two years prior to Scottie's death. A nurse from the AIDS clinic told me one day that as mother of an AIDS patient and wife of an Alzheimer's patient, I had drawn two of the worst diseases known to modern man in terms of long-term suffering for both patient and family. A doctor at an Alzheimer's clinic in Birmingham, Alabama, told me that 60 percent of the caregivers die before the patients. Having to drive to Birmingham, an unfamiliar city in a different state, and find my way when I had no idea of where the office would be within the huge complex of buildings, was overwhelming. Things that might seem small, like finally being able to get Mr. Ralph's car keys so that he could no longer drive, were huge. What a sad day, to see such an outstanding, strong man have to forfeit the keys to his pickup.

On one occasion in the hospital in Memphis, I was told to go to another office to pick up some records while they had Mr. Ralph in an examination room. I had put great stress on them not leaving him alone. When I came back, he was gone. They had no idea where he was. It required a great deal of discipline not to have a fit over them being so irresponsible. Here I was at a hospital, and my Alzheimer's husband was wandering around and could be anywhere—including outside in the parking lot or the street. I looked all around the nearby halls and then went back to the department that I had been sent to, to see if possibly someone had attempted to bring him to where I was supposed to have been sent. My heart was racing and I was near panic, but all the while I appealed to God in prayer and request. My next move was to go back to the ground floor to find the security office and to put out an all-points bulletin, giving the description of a man that would probably match a thousand others at the hospital. I had been on the floor of the doctor's office, on the floor of the other department, and back to both again, and I had pushed the button for the elevator to go down to the ground floor. The elevator door opened, and there stood Mr. Ralph. He looked at me and said, as God is my witness, "Where in the world have you been?" My gratitude to God and my relief were overwhelming.

These are just tiny examples, considering that Mr. Ralph had Alzheimer's for a total of twelve years before he died and Scottie had AIDS for four, suffering terribly during the last three years. I am not in any way looking for pity, but I need to use this testimony to show what a friend Jesus is to me—how He prepared me before, kept me during, and brought me through so much. Simultaneously, it shows that Satan hopes for our destruction. Having strength and conviction in your trust in God far beyond what is normal or average is imperative, if you are to be able to keep your eye on the prize and fulfill God's purpose for your life. Had I not had the strength provided by God, there were times when I could have registered anger off the scale by the ignorance and noncompassionate behavior of people toward Scottie. People sometimes tell me that I am just different, but they say it in a positive way. I have decided it's the way troubles look after they've been yielded to the Master's hand. No matter how low or incapable I had felt at times during those terrible years, I never doubted God—myself, yes, but not Him—and He has never let me down. I do not say that I always understood, but that is not the important part. As a child might not understand why he needs to eat vegetables, so must a child of God obey the authority of power in his or her life.

Dealing with the weight of rejection from the "Christian" community during all that time was very painful. Where the Bible says we are to count it all joy when trials come, it means that we are being presented with another opportunity with which we can prove our loyalty to God. James 1:2–8 (Amp) says, "Consider it wholly joyful, my brethren, whenever you are enveloped in or encounter trials of any sort, or fall into various temptations. Be assured and understand that the trial and proving of your faith bring out endurance and steadfastness and patience. But let endurance and steadfastness and patience have full play and do a thorough work, so that you may be [people] perfectly and fully developed (with no defects), lacking in nothing. If any of you is deficient in wisdom let him ask of the giving God [Who gives] to every one liberally and ungrudgingly, without reproaching or faultfinding, and it will be given him. Only it must be in faith that he asks, with no wavering—no hesitating no doubting. For the one who wavers (hesitates, doubts) is like the billowing surge out at sea, that is blown hither and thither and tossed by the wind. For truly, let not such a person imagine that he will receive anything [he asks for] from the Lord, [For being as he is] a man of two minds—hesitating, dubious, irresolute—[he is] unstable and unreliable and uncertain about everything (he thinks, feels, decides)."

I believe that many have looked at Job incorrectly. Nearly everybody always says, "Poor old Job," but I believe the more accurate attitude should be Hurrah for Job. He didn't just squeak by on the test by waiting it out, just hoping to survive. He kept trying, loved God, and responded appropriately to the test. I truly believe that the Book of Job is not just for us to see that he was sorely tested and managed to survive, but is intended for us to gain a lesson about how to live a life on this earth. Job's experience was a condensed version of an example of life being a test that only faith, obedience, and loyalty will overcome. Job was loyal to God. Satan was allowed to test Job's genuineness, and every aspect of Job's life was affected. Job kept trying, but not always correctly. Nobody gets it all right all of the time except God. Regarding Job 29 (Amp), there is a footnote that reads, "Blameless and upright" as Job had been—and God had so pronounced him—his *misunderstood* afflictions had caused him to get dangerously off center. Instead of keeping his mind stayed on God and justifying Him, he is giving his whole thought to justifying himself. Instead of humility there is only self-righteousness. In this chapter he used pronouns referring to himself *fifty* times. But when he was able to see himself as God saw him, he loathed himself and repented "in dust and ashes" (emphasis added). God restored everything and more.

The things neither of earth nor of the flesh were the focus or the subject of the test, though man is inclined to look at all that was taken away, and at how good Job was. The value at risk was Job's (and our) spiritual life versus human priorities. One has and one has not produced behavior that is refined and approved by

God. Each of us is dealt with individually, according to our own purpose and destiny in life. Scottie's and Mr. Ralph's situations concerned theirs. God had put me in their lives to have faith for their healing, to love and pray for them, and to offer comfort as much as possible. After they were gone, my role was to respond through acceptance of, and in reaction to, the fate of people I had been given to love. Someday we will each leave someone else who has to deal with losing us. It may not be intended specifically for them to benefit from, but it will be a time when they can show God that they trust Him with the future.

The intent of this book is to give God glory and honor, to explain how He can work through any kind of circumstances to bring us into victory. Jesus was with us through it all, and because He is the power that provided the success, it is necessary that His hand be held right along with the telling of the challenges. Satan's activity is always followed by God defeating him, if we understand what God expects us to say or do. I would not want to put too much emphasis on the problem, thus allowing Satan to feel good about himself, without putting the real emphasis on the Holy Spirit—who is our "comforter (counselor, helper, intercessor, advocate, strengthener, standby) whom the Father will send" in Jesus's name, according to John 14:26 (Amp).

On one occasion, a young preacher from another town saw our motor home on the side of the highway beside our land. He stopped to greet us and to see if we were interested in visiting his church. It was not only several miles away, it was also a denomination that was selective in the parts of the Bible they chose to practice. I do not believe that he expected us to attend after our conversation revealed that we leaned toward the extreme in believing God's Word. No other preacher from the nearby area came to our door for more than ten years. We really weren't welcome there.

I do want to say something good about our neighboring area, though. I can't say that they welcomed us or treated us with love, and I never got to know any of them well enough to say anything personal about them during all my years of hardship in their community. I don't intend to make something up, but this I will say: I feel sure that there were a lot of good and caring hearts who just didn't know us or understand us. We were outsiders and city folks to them, and their lot was cast according to their understanding—or lack of it. So by God's grace, I forgive them and wish them the best. I will also say that one of the hardest lessons in life has been to reconcile pain with forgiveness. It's not the same as someone just calling you a name. But obey God because it can be done, and you'll be better off for forgiving others. The peace that I live with is well worth the price of obedience, and even more so, because I felt a little defiant and didn't really want to obey at the time. It's an even higher price for us to pay when we have to wrench it out of ourselves, but God knows and appreciates our effort when it hasn't come easy for us. He says, "What is it to your credit if you only do what everybody else does?" So reach farther, climb higher. Let your little light shine! Blessings come to a wounded heart that forgives.

***

A Tribute to Scottie

He came into this world on the Lord's Day in November 1959. His spirit went back to be with Jesus, also on the Lord's Day in April 1994. In his early adulthood, he did not live his life for God, but during his last years he became dedicated toward changing from a child of God into a servant of God. Because he had lived away from home for many years, I do not know the exact time and place where he turned it all over to God. I just know that when he had reached the point of being ill and then returned home, he had a very repentant heart. Once he had told me, with tears flowing, that Satan had had such a grip on his life for a while, that he could hardly bear to remember some of the terrible things he had done. I believed him to be referring to the months and years after he had moved away from home, after his dad ordered him out of the house when Scottie had confessed tendencies toward wrong behavior—which I had taken as a plea for help. He was eighteen years old. He disappeared into the night, and we did not hear from him again for six months. I had tried to stop him from leaving on that terrible night, but tempers were high and emotions were out of control. I could not stop the forceful nature of two men who were in angry conflict. Scottie had his car but no money, no job, and no home outside of ours. I cannot dwell further on that fateful night, or on the heartbreak and consequences that followed, but I can tell you that that sort of family scene should *never* occur, and people with God in their lives are much more able to cope with difficult emotional trials. First of all, they try to love and help each other, and with God's help, order returns and people become healed from those demonic attacks. True believers know that the human before them is not the real enemy; Satan, operating in or through them, is. God's Word is clear on how to get rid of his torment and restore peace.

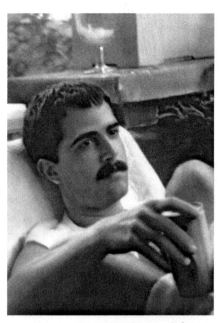

Scott – contemplating life

However, the lives that were touched and the lessons that were learned through the price Scottie paid have had far-reaching effects. He had hoped to be healed, have a wife and children, and live a normal life. Instead, he received the greatest healing of all. He was delivered from worldly concerns. The illness placed him in a position that really made his life count through testimony and ministry. Through nearly three years of hospital stays, clinic visits, and waiting rooms, we were able to share the love of Jesus and the hope of glory. We called it our "waiting room" ministry.

Scottie and I were often so very alone during the terribleness and devastation of his physical illness. Many medical professionals treated him with fear and ignorance concerning his disease. Certainly some family members and friends did. During one really low, sad time, while we were experiencing one of the many scares with him at death's door, I stayed beside him day and night. I felt deserted, heartbroken, and more or less abandoned, except for God. The hospital was near downtown Memphis, and Memphis has an extremely high crime rate. I was a long way from my home on the river, more than one hundred miles. I can only remember two visits (for which we were very grateful) from family and friends who actually lived in Memphis—during all the time we spent at that hospital—and this time was no different. I pictured them at their homes, watching TV and going about as though everything was just fine. I looked around the cold hospital room and at all the machinery hooked up to my son, knowing that his last breath could be at any time. I did not want to sleep in case he had any sort of need that I could help with, or in case he might utter a soft word or look toward me with a little smile. This poem came to my mind.

I've seen my son nearing Heaven's gate,
And heard demons rattling chains from hell.
But through it all, and up till now,
I know our Jesus will prevail.

The thought my heart yearns to convey
Concerns not the answer, but the test.
Bitterness, hurt, resentment comes;
Prayer, repentance—getting no rest.

And the excuses I hear from others
Over why they can't do that or this,
Reveal the power of Satan
Through the spirit of selfishness.

I don't expect the world to stop
Because of Scottie and me.
I just wish folks would imagine our pain,
Then act accordingly.

It's how we show love for each other
That reveals the heart within.
It's who sticks closer than a brother
Who shows himself a true friend.

So the test that is really before me
(Please pray that I'll succeed!)
Is to forgive those who claim to love me—
While they ignore my greatest need.

Praise the mighty God, we were able to forgive all who
shunned Scottie or acted hypocritically. There is a simple fact here:
if we don't forgive others, God doesn't forgive us (Matt. 6:14–15),
so forgiving is definitely necessary and worth doing.

The ones who did bless us with their love, kindness, and
understanding became prized with great value to our hearts.
Scottie's nurse, Marsha Jo Harris, was one precious prize, a rarity
indeed. She was just beginning a new job in home health care and
came regularly to visit him. Her compassionate, valiant young
heart caused her to question the stigma of ignorance surrounding

the disease. Because of her joyful, radiant spirit, she made Scottie's last few months blessed beyond measure. She laughed with us, cried with us, and sincerely loved us, while never missing a beat concerning his medical care. I know beyond the shadow of a doubt that God sent her to us. She will, for the rest of her days, strive to educate people concerning the pitifulness and devastation of AIDS; that you can't catch it just by being around a person with it, and that good, praying Christian families can also be touched by its merciless tentacles of death.

Even if victims aren't Christians (yet), your job from God's point of view is to love, pity, and care about their suffering. Use God's tenderness and grace to open the door for them to receive God's love and salvation. That's called responding to the call of a hurting world. That's called doing good to all and sharing the Gospel. That's called the righteousness of Jesus coming forth through a mere human, impacting people's lives so that they can live in eternal victory. That's called exciting, wonderful, spirit-filled living—go for it! Nothing this world has to offer can even come close to the wonder of being in the family of God, or of knowing that you played a part in someone's deliverance or salvation.

See how the ripples from your personal little pebble in the pond can just go on and on and on. See how living by God's way can have such a wonderful effect on others, as Marsha and Scott's did.

I remember so well a cold winter night in Memphis, when Scottie, Mr. Ralph, and I had stopped at the Krystal Burger on our way home. Scottie had had chemotherapy, and it was unusual for him to be willing to eat after the treatments. He had become so skinny that I would have braved most anything to get calories into him. As we stood in line, a black man approached me and asked for money. I responded that if he was hungry, he could order anything he wanted, and I would pay for it. He was happy with that, and we all placed our orders. As we turned to sit down, I said to him that we would like for him to sit with us. He seemed surprised but agreed. After a few minutes of small talk, I asked him this question: "Just say, for instance, that Jesus came back to earth this very minute, suddenly appearing, splitting the eastern sky, and coming to take His family out of here because it was time for the end-times to begin. Would you be ready?" He said he didn't know. We all talked together for a while, and Scottie was good at explaining things, which he did regarding the Rapture of the Church. The man showed a sensitive heart, and we asked if he would like to be saved and to say the sinner's prayer, and he said he would. It was a blessing to all, and a very sweet moment. Then Scottie reached into his pocket and took out all the money that he had, which was only a handful of coins, and said, "This is all the money that I have, but it is enough to do you some good if tomorrow you buy a newspaper and find yourself a job. We'll be praying that you do." Hope was born in that man that night.

That's one testimony of Scottie's walk with God, actually displaying the appropriate Christian attributes through action and not mere words, not only blessing our personal lives but expanding on that learning experience by growing with more knowledge and love—and then passing it on. Just think about your attitude, priorities, actions, and dedication to God; the Holy Bible; what kind of testimony folks receive from the way you act; and the impact you leave behind. Many testimonies won't even be good, much less glorious. Reach for it, folks. It won't make you strange (as the world may think); it will make you walk with the extraordinary, be useful to the Kingdom of God, and bless your fellowman. Now how can you resist?

***

Regardless of my pain, trials, and victories, life did not stop and wait for me. I do not casually go from my son's or husband's death to another subject with disrespect. But we can't make life stop and wait for us, and the challenges just kept coming. Some trials may not be very interesting, but because of the length of their duration or the battleground before victory, they become unusual, something not experienced before, and they were tremendous difficulties to have to deal with during those years in my personal wilderness. They were tough challenges that addressed character, patience, endurance, and long-suffering. I would ask Mr. Ralph to pray with me, and he would as well as he could. I do not believe that his faith was negatively affected so long as he was able to understand the challenge.

I knew that it was my responsibility to stay engaged in the management of our financial interests, and to be strong and have enough faith to continue with the other necessary aspects of life. Mr. Ralph was unable to help me other than joining me in prayer. There were times when he would put on every hat he owned at one time and walk up and down the hall at midnight. On another occasion he woke me, standing over me. When I opened my eyes, he said, "Just what on earth do you think you are doing?" If I tried to give him medication or vitamins, sometimes he would say, "I'm not taking that. I know what you are trying to do." None of these things are a bad report about a precious soul; I tell it to reveal some of the confusion that was constant.

Somehow I had managed to navigate my way through the purchase of another piece of real estate that many people had told me would be a waste of money. It was three hundred acres of wooded land adjacent to our original purchase of the fifty-four acres, and it ran nearly a mile along the Tennessee River. Older family members, who were reputed to know about land values, said that it was just old undeveloped, useless land that nobody had ever wanted and nobody ever would. I have to admit that spending our retirement savings was not such an easy thing to do, but I really felt that God was urging me to pursue. It took three years to close the purchase on that property. I stopped seeking anyone else's advice and went with God on it; He always knows what's best. It was definitely the right thing to do and generated a lot of blessings. He knew that I was, and would continue to be, a cheerful giver. That victory put wind in my sails and helped so much to refresh my soul. Something positive had happened. Whatever the world around me continued to do to bring about my failure, God prevailed. Having said that, please understand that "the world" is Satan's domain, and people are often cooperating with his influence against God's children even without knowing it. I never thought that anybody was out to get me except Satan. He was using every wile of the devil that he could, and any mouth that would cooperate with his negative, thoughtless, selfish, grasping agenda of destruction against a claim of faith.

I had always heard the expression that facing certain difficulties was like fighting city hall. I can attest to that. I literally had to fight city hall for city water to be provided for my family. There was a tiny town several miles from us, and "city" was their word, not mine. There were farms that had city water running to their barns for herds of cattle from that water supply—but they wouldn't allow us to have it. I remember one day when we were in court, there were eight men dressed in suits looking very intimidating on the city's side of the courtroom. On my side was me, one small female reporter from a nearby town, and my husband with Alzheimer's. And of course, God was there! He is the final judge, and He will always cause His children to prevail if their cause is just. This wasn't a simple problem; my face had been seen on TV more than once, as well as in the newspapers, over the opposing point that I had taken against city hall. It didn't increase my family's popularity with the local people. They and their livestock, and even one personally owned golf course that needed water for their greens, already had city water. That very nerve-racking, emotionally charged subject remained with stubborn persistence. At one point, I was given a date on which I would be arrested and put in jail if I did not submit to their demand. I told them that I was sorry; but that my family included a small child (Greg's daughter, Rebecca) and a sick man (Mr. Ralph), and that they could not be deprived of water when herds of livestock had access to it. I told them that if they were going to take me to jail, that would be okay, as long as they would allow Mr. Ralph to be in the cell with me because he was totally dependent on me and was always concerned when he couldn't see me. The kind judge cancelled the idea of arrest.

While that court case was going on, it was necessary to also stand in faith for the proposed new bridge over the Tennessee River to be built near our newly purchased property. The bridge was rumored to be built somewhere in our area and would certainly improve property values. Of course God knows the before and after of everybody's dealings. Al Gore's uncle owned property on the river not far from us. Every time I said I was standing in faith for the new bridge to be built near our property, the response was always that the location chosen would be on Al Gore's uncle's property. It really became tiresome. Finally I started saying, "Well, if you want to be a name dropper, I know God." It wasn't arrogance; it was truly what I depended upon. The power of God wasn't affected by people's politics, and the new bridge now stands on the property adjacent to the land we had purchased. Our land prices soared. Isn't God amazing and wonderful? He is so great and faithful to His Word. These things are not told as any credit to me, or in pride—except for a pride in God. I tell it as an example and an encouragement to others. It's my witness to how He has kept His word to me. He can't work through you if you don't trust Him. Just make sure it's His guidance, and not just something worldly you want. Prayer and time with Him will reveal it to you. Nobody said that a faith walk would always be easy, but it sure is productive and exciting, and it most certainly works.

After the new bridge was finished, there was an opening ceremony. High officials from the state were expected, as well as the press. We were still involved in the effort to get city water for our family, and you cannot possibly imagine the strength I had to have from God to force myself to take my husband, my seven-year-old granddaughter, and a picket sign saying "WE NEED WATER" to the grand opening.

> **My face glowed red, I am certain, as I walked and stood with my big sign. I am naturally somewhat shy and quite cowardly in large groups of people. God has taught me that there are things beyond myself that are worth fighting for. I stood my ground and was able to do so only because I knew that He was with me.**

A very high state official had his limousine stop beside me so that he could inquire about what I was doing and why. I asked him why they were making such a big commotion over their great achievement of having the bridge in that location if their claim was that it would bring progress and revenue to both the state and county. I asked who they were going to get to move there if there was no drinking water for people's homes. There was the expense of drilling in limestone rock, which was everywhere along the river bank properties, and nearly all the wells around there contained sulfur. I asked him what he thought of city people wanting to build there if they had to drill, not certain of how deep, or how great the cost—or whether water would even be found at the site they had chosen. I asked if he really thought that city ladies wanted their homes and laundry to smell like sulfur; if he thought they would want to drink sulfur water or have it ruin all their plumbing and fixtures. I also mentioned the high cost and risks of trying to clean up river water enough for household use, and I asked him if he knew that there was a higher risk of cancer for people in that area who used river water for their homes. I honestly do not believe that any state officials who were involved in the politics and revenue end of things even *knew* that there was no water for their real estate "progress." The official granted me an appointment.

In my effort to get water for us (having nothing to do with progress for the state), I had contacted every politician I could remember the name of—more than once, including the governor's office. They were "sympathetic" but not willing to use their official power to dictate to a small-town mayor, his councilmen, and city attorney. On the surface, this politician didn't work out, either. However, he had offered to hear what we had to say, and he had given us an appointment to see him at his office. I contribute our obtaining water to God and God alone.

For reasons known only to God, after we had sat down for the appointment, the official asked me if I was a Christian, to which I said, "Yes, sir."

He looked at my husband and said to him, "Is she spirit-filled?" My husband was no longer able to participate normally in conversations at that point of the illness, so he didn't answer. The man asked him again. Mr. Ralph was confused and thought the man was angry at him, so big tears started running down his face.

I was stunned at the official's questions and then at his absurd behavior. I said, "Why are you causing him to cry? I told you that we are dealing with Alzheimer's." He replied that he often didn't have much patience about things and that maybe I could pray for him sometime. I said, "What about now?" Surprisingly, he agreed, and so I did. I walked behind his chair, put my hand on his shoulder, and prayed. Afterward, we talked about the water situation briefly, with him telling me that he couldn't interfere with the city's business, either.

As my husband and I went to the door to leave, the man said to me, "Maybe you were sent here today to pray for this old man," referring to himself.

I answered, "Well, it doesn't appear that I achieved my goal with this visit, but I would just as readily have come for your reason too—and actually would rather have." And that was the truth. I had gotten over my protective little flare of anger toward the man for his insensitive behavior to my husband's kind and gentle soul, and I honestly did pray for him with sincerity and love for another of God's children. Little flares of anger are one of the sins that so easily beset me. (Little flares—where does that sound like it comes from?) Even though perfection in this life is unattainable, I am sorry when I react poorly and in an un-Christ-like manner. I have added this part of our story simply because it shows just what extraordinary, unexpected situations came against my senses and my faith. These situations were so challenging, with doors that were practically nailed shut, and pushed emotional stress and physical exhaustion to record-breaking levels at times. There is no way on this earth that any of these things could have been achieved except through the mighty God of heaven and earth.

The whole business about the city water was finally resolved in our favor, as I knew by faith that it would be, and now where city water had never been provided before, it was readily available to a growing community. That ordeal lasted about three years, and I find it amazing that so many of my trials, and maybe those of other people too, have been about the same length of time as Jesus's ministry time on this earth. Bless His holy name, still again. It is to God's credit that that area now has city water.

These trials were happening simultaneously, or at least overlapping. My family must have achieved a lot of good with that wonderful bookstore ministry, because the enemy really came after us with his most wicked bag of tricks.

My dear aunt died, followed by my stepfather. There were three rattlesnake bites to family dogs, resulting in one death. One of our little Eskimo Spitz dogs, named Ruthie, was viciously attacked by coyotes. What a frightful, pitiful sight. She was pure white and there was so much blood. She spent two weeks at the vet clinic and then another two weeks indoors to recover enough to go out without help. Praise God, she did fully recover, except for one droopy little ear—it just made her look sweeter—and she lived to be about fifteen years old. The devil didn't really get away with a thing, because ministry resulted from all his dirty deeds. Our God truly reigns. I was weak but God was strong. Yes, Jesus loves me and you. When adversity comes, the anchor holds. One of my dear friends says the word "can't" is not in my vocabulary.

Why should it be, if God is with me? I used to tell my children that I had read in a psychology book that the word "can't" really means "I don't want to." Building a stronger relationship with God emerges from the pain of trials when you have determinedly kept your trust in Him, no matter what.

And now for the big question. If we believe in God's healing power, why didn't my son and husband get healed? That I cannot answer in the way one might want to hear. I only know this: God has His overall plan and has a different and higher view of things than we do. We are looking at a loved *one*, while He is looking after all of us. There is no telling what the weaving of a heavenly tapestry looks like, but I'm sure it's beyond belief. The big events in a person's life, like birth, marriage, and death, affect many. Each and every person has his own very personal relationship with God, and we each deal directly with Him.

> **Each of us will undoubtedly leave a course of events that will follow our departure. They will take off and have their effect as a follow-up after we're gone. It's a big responsibility to know that you will still be influencing lives according to what you did before you physically died. I pray that I may cause no pain. Life is of great value and counts for more than we give it credit for. Consider how you live, because it's not just about you. Death, and sometimes the time leading up to it or after it, makes changes that can have far-reaching results.**

I know that the waiting-room ministry with Scottie, and the giving away of hundreds of Christian books and Bibles in Mr. Ralph's and Scottie's honor, are still rippling little waves across the ministry pond, going on and on and on. My heart chose to participate in the effectiveness of their love for God and in the effectiveness of the lives of these two precious souls—and I'm sure that that was part of God's plan too, giving us all the privilege of participating in more and more of sharing His message of hope and love together.

We must consider that the very personal aspect of physical death must be influenced by the heart and soul of the person, and by his or her private relationship with God. Perhaps when a Christian is at the point of death, his or her thoughts may be different than what we think they might be. Sometimes people don't feel worthy because of something in their past. God always forgives when sincerely asked, but some people just don't feel deserving, and their faith is affected. Some may simply be tired and want to go on to be with Him, especially if they have been strong believers and are really looking forward to the experience of Heaven; others sometimes just give up the fight. Whatever the case may be, because of my love for God, I do believe that when the individual and God are looking directly at each other, the soul—the immaterial essence—of the human is greatly comforted with the encounter. It understands what is going to happen, it has no fear, is willing to go, and nothing is left to guesswork. Sadness, confusion, and all other negatives are gone at that point, and only a happy agreement with great anticipation and joy are left to be fulfilled. It will be okay; the anchor holds. How often have we heard that someone smiled as life left the body?

When Scottie died, I lifted my face toward my Father and said, "Thank You, Lord, for receiving my precious son unto Yourself. I know where he is now, and I know I'll see him later. He is in a new city, but I'll be going to the same city eventually, and I'll see him when I get there. Thank You, Lord, for sharing him with me while he was on this earth. I loved him dearly, and I love You." Now the truth of the matter was this: what I wanted to do at the same time was die too—or at the very least to fall face-down on the floor, beating my fists against the floor and screaming in complete despair. My soul guided me toward the witness that I needed to portray for my younger, also very precious son, Greg, and for my sick husband's benefit. One was heartbroken and had just witnessed the passing of his brother; the other was worried, childlike, and anxious. My soul convinced my body to do the right thing. When I called his nurse to tell her, her immediate reply was, "Well, he beat us to the prize," which I knew to be true. I was so blessed to be able to deal with the spirit of grief by relying on God's Word about where saints go when the body dies. "To be absent from the body is to be present with the Lord" (2 Cor. 5:8, NKJV). That is such a great comfort. Those words are on Scottie's headstone, and they are the reason that he's not there.

It was the same when my husband went to glory. He had died in a hospital, where he had been for five days in a coma with pneumonia. Except for running home once for a short time one afternoon to get more clothes, I stayed by his side day and night. He also moved on into glory and into the loving arms of God. A little girl at his funeral said, "Well, Miss Dian, I guess he's singing and dancing with the angels right now." Out of the mouths of babes, peace came to me, and again the anchor held.

Anyone losing a loved one should never picture that person in the grave. It will absolutely wreck your emotions if you allow the spirit of grief to cause you to do that. They are not in the grave. One of the enormous benefits to being a Christian is to know where you will be directly upon your physical death. I forced every thought like that into submission, into seeing Scottie sitting at the feet of Jesus, talking and joyful, and then later I pictured Mr. Ralph with Jesus too, but singing and also joyful, because gospel music was one of his greatest pleasures.

Both of these men were healed in the most ultimate way. I don't want to think that my faith would be criticized, and neither should anyone have a wrong kind of pride about how well they could have handled things. There was pain, regret, guilt, depression, and an onslaught of other negative feelings pulling me under, but the fine threads of gold woven through my soul, along with His tremendous love, gently pulled me back up into God's grace. If we are trying our hardest, with multiple high-pressure issues going on, I do not believe that God will allow one person to die just because someone else may not have risen to the occasion.

Ultimately it is in God's hands, and He knows our hearts. I am glad that His great heart is so kind. I wish that people would be kinder to one another.

Sometimes it's just not in the overall plan for one to remain. However, we have to give it all we've got every time in praying for him or her, because any time may be the time that your faith is an act of the fulfilling of one of your purposes in life. So try hard every time, and don't be discouraged and say, "I tried, but it just didn't work." We don't know what worked. Oftentimes it does work in visible ways, so we don't want to be found slacking just in case it is one of those times. That person's destiny is still in God's hands. Besides, I personally saw the quantity and quality of ministry that touched other people's lives after these two were safely home. To say that you followed all the rules, and the one being prayed for was a good Christian but he or she died anyway, is to compare you and the sick person's righteousness to God's, and having Him come out as the unrighteous one. Surely no one thinks like that, that your prayer and the dying one's righteousness were fine, so God must not have been righteous. Think that over.

Isaiah 57:1–2 (Amp) is comforting: "The righteous man perishes, and no one lays it to heart; and merciful and devout men are taken away, none considering that the uncompromisingly upright and godly person is taken away from the calamity and evil to come—even through wickedness. He [in death] enters into peace."

I would like to present one more thought on this subject. One's physical death doesn't look the same to God as it does to us. To us it is the great loss of a loved one, and we will miss having him or her accessible to us. To God, it's a continuation of the spirit of one of His people (if he or she is saved) coming back into glory with Him. We're just going through a "training program" on the earth. He gives us life; we learn about Him, become immersed in His character, and then return to Him. From the human perspective, those who die are gone. To Him, they have returned home. Psalm 116:15 says, "Precious in the sight of the Lord is the death of his saints." If we would see the spiritual reality of what we think of as death, and see it as the spirit proceeding on into the wondrous life hereafter, how could we be so sad? Fear and superstition have caused us to view it as final—when life has only just begun. Think about this and take comfort in God's Word: He isn't going to disappoint us at the end; He's proven Himself too many times, and He loves us. If we and our loved ones want to have a happy reunion together someday, everybody needs to be born again, from above. His blood purchased our right to live forever.

I have wondered how God handles situations where some of His children may be praying for the person to be healed, in Jesus's name, and others of different denominations are asking God to just let the suffering person go on home. I'm confident that He deals with the life and soul of the suffering person because it is his or her life and soul and future. We all have to swim upstream sometimes, don't we, by praying in opposite directions than other Christians.

After Scottie died, his nurse, Marsha, accompanied me, and we spoke to youth church groups, helping them to understand how you could and could not catch AIDS. Our focus was also about the kind of behavior and attitude a Christian should demonstrate both to an AIDS victim and the victim's family. After that, I spoke to people employed in the medical profession for more than a year, in Jackson, Tennessee, mainly regarding the Christian perspective. I also visited an AIDS victim regularly in his home for approximately a year, until he died.

The Christmas after Scottie died, I obtained special permission from the AIDS clinic to visit a ward of a large hospital in Memphis on Christmas Day. Roger (a friend then, my friend and husband now) went with me. On the three-hour drive there, I had spiritual music playing and was praying. There was no unnecessary conversation; I wanted my spirit and soul to be tuned in to God when I got there. As mentioned already, Scottie and I had done a lot of waiting-room ministry during his doctor visits—some welcome and effective, some not. On that Christmas Day, we took very nice gift bags, which our whole family had prepared that also included beautiful Christian Christmas cards of hope and love. At each of the fifteen doors, we asked patients if it would be okay to bring them a gift bag that contained an assortment of items, including a Christian book filled with promises from God. I don't feel comfortable trying to trick people into hearing about our mighty God. If they have the idea up-front, I think they will have more regard for what I have to say, and they will not be so defensive. It seemed like the more loving way to approach and respect people, especially those who were so ill.

At the first room we entered, there was a man named Willie. We said hello and talked with him for a few minutes, and then, without having a clue as to exactly what to do or how it would be received, I mentioned the book of *Promises from God* in the gift bag. I explained to him that they weren't just nice sayings but were real promises from our God, and that they were more valuable than money in the bank. Then I asked if he had ever thought much about Heaven. He said that he had been wondering a lot about it but didn't know whether he would go there. I explained the plan of salvation, including repentance, as we talked for a while, and then I asked him if he wanted to ask Jesus into his heart, repent, and ask for forgiveness of his sins, and if he wanted to be sure that he would go to Heaven. He said yes to that, and he certainly seemed sincere, so I took hold of his hand and knelt beside his bed and prayed. He followed with his own words and heart. Afterward I asked him if he now felt certain about Heaven, and he smiled and said that he did. I did not ask Willie personal questions about how he contracted the disease; that was between Willie and God. My joy and my job were to bring spiritual refreshing to his soul and body.

Since I have told you that we were visiting an AIDS ward of the hospital, some might make wrong assumptions. Having dealt with an AIDS patient for three years, plus spent some ministry time after Scottie died, I had consequently spent many hours of many days hearing and observing the usual reactions to the opinions of the rest of the human race—with the harshest coming from professing Christians. As with many people who are sick with all sorts of diseases all over the world, most do not know Jesus *as the Healer,* and so I have a heart of compassion for the spiritual and physical dilemma of a person with AIDS. I can tell you in all honesty that most people make an immediate, unfair judgment call based on the stigma surrounding the disease. Please don't stumble spiritually by thinking that the fifteen people we visited that day were all homosexuals, or drug users—or that even if they were, don't think that homosexuals can't be forgiven or saved (as I have heard expressed before). Romans chapter one describes God's Word on the subject of homosexuality, but His Word also describes many sins with similar consequences in other places of His Word. Look at the whole picture and pray people out of hell, not into it. God is watching our every move too, and we are depending on His grace, aren't we?

Also, please don't think that if we led anyone to the Lord that day and then they passed away before they were water baptized, that they couldn't go to Heaven because of having not been water baptized. Like the thief on the cross who accepted Jesus and then went to Heaven the same day as when he died on the cross beside Jesus, God's grace covers all. If we only had His power without His kindness, love, and grace, we would be in a scary situation. The truth of His Word says that what He will do for one, He will do for all (Gal. 2:6, NKJV). If the thief was allowed to go to Heaven when he was a dying man and had no opportunity to follow through with water baptism, then another dying person would be given that same grace, if they had both met the requirements of spiritual baptism. This is another instance where the two main uses of the word "baptized" are muddled by humans. It should be acknowledged that the thief on the cross had been spiritually baptized into Jesus because he had sincerely recognized and accepted Him as Lord. That is the first determining factor. If you limit God concerning others while allowing yourself to enter in, then that's on your record with God, not the other (repentant) sinner's record. But honestly, that would be like shutting the door to Heaven in someone's face. How could a Christian do that? Matthew 12:31 (Amp) tells us that every sin and every evil can be forgiven except blasphemy against the Holy Spirit. Most people who get saved in church wait days and sometimes weeks, or maybe even months, before a water baptism service occurs. Do you think that after they have repented sincerely, believed wholeheartedly, and were spiritually saved, that if they died during the time between their acceptance of Christ and their water baptism, their soul would be refused at Heaven's gate? Surely not. It is His will for everybody to be saved, and He says that the way to be saved is to be spiritually born again from above. One very important thought that would be suggested here is to realize that the King James Version, as well as others, usually use the word baptize without distinguishing between the two primary biblical meanings of spiritual or physical baptism. When reading the Bible, please stay alert to which meaning the writer is most likely referring. The use of footnotes and commentaries can be so helpful when it hasn't been made clear.

We left Willie smiling, and I can honestly say that was the best Christmas gift that I have ever had in my entire life. I will never forget it, I thank God for it, and it was, in my heart, for the glory of God and in Scottie's honor. Being able to participate in that was one of the most shining moments of my life. Thank you, Jesus, for showing me another blessing that resulted from Scottie having left early, which helped Willie before it was too late.

After Mr. Ralph died, I opened a small Christian bookstore in a town that was twenty miles from my rural home. I knew that I had to do something that was ministry related for the sake of honoring him. I put ads about the store in two or three newspapers around the area that read, "If you have a need, God has the answer—and if you don't have a Bible, we'll give you one." And we did. It was a great year, with many conversations about the Word and the power and the love of God—and it was joyfully healing to me. By intending to give, I abundantly received. We gave away promise books to everybody who wanted one, as well as a variety of other books as the situation required. I still have boxes of Christian books and Bibles on hand, and I will continue to give them to folks for as long as I live on this earth.

God is so kind and good. The other day, I said in frustration that I wished that I would never sin again, and if I got under the bed, maybe I could avoid sinning. I knew that was useless, though, because I would just have had a bad thought! So to the best of my knowledge, we really can't find any place to hide or to get away from ourselves, which is why God is so awesome—He loves us anyway. He says that when we ask and receive forgiveness, then He forgets the sin. I guess we can't and don't forget it, because we need it as a reminder of our "what not to do" list, especially if it did bring us shame and pain, or even worse, if it had a negative effect on our testimony. By the way, remembering lessons doesn't mean that you can't forgive yourself, as God does and as He wants us to do, so that we *can* live with peace in our hearts. If we don't have peace, then we need to increase our faith. Faith in His grace, love, and forgiveness will cause peace to come to you.

Can't you see that crimson stream of blood that He shed to atone for our sins? There's a lot of blood in the human body, and His flowed from Calvary, draining His body when He had done no wrong, so that we who do wrong so often can be cleansed and made white as new fallen snow, so that we each can be presented as a member of His church and can be accepted into the family of God. I am constantly concerned that people just don't show Him nearly enough gratitude or appreciation when He is so very worthy. If church seems like a duty to you, you don't have the right attitude. Please give Him honor and respect. Give some serious thought about what He has done for you—not for me, but for you personally. Let Him know that you are grateful and that you love Him.

All accolades go to Him, who is the one who will show us the way, bring us through, and take care of us—if we will just listen to Him. Don't be a hearer only, but one who will hear and *do*. Wouldn't it be something if we could go back in time to the way things were when Jesus physically walked the earth? Wouldn't that draw a crowd of folks to share the Gospel with? People are so needful of healing in their souls and bodies. Folks are reluctant to listen unless we can communicate the power of His blood over their current situation. Ours is not a mystical, old-fashioned disconnect with reality, as many people think. We need to show love, be glad to be Christians, stop criticizing each other, and act like true believers with joy in our hearts and a ready prayer of faith. Act like you know that if the Bible says it, it is guaranteed by the blood of Jesus. That includes miracles too, folks. God's power is activated by our faith, and since salvation includes being saved, healed, and delivered, we need to go about with the signs of miracles and answered prayer following us—signs and wonders, signs of *salvation, healing, and deliverance*—which are miracles. Probably one of the top needs today is for hope, as well as the knowledge that God is real, has power, and is on His children's side! Jesus can give people that, if someone will just tell them about Him. Faith-filled prayers that display His power at work are a great testimony. The truth is that we should and could be going about Jesus's business like they did during the days when He physically walked the earth. Only *we* are different; He changeth not.

This tiny portion of my life, and the responses that have kept me in His care (by my having the heart to try to do things His way), is not written down to lift me up. I could have done things far better and in a far more excellent way, but He worked with what I submitted to His guidance, and this is a good place to say that we are our own worst enemies when we don't submit ourselves totally to Him. This is also a testimony about faith giving you victory and empowerment over the devil, through Christ. It's about tithing and seeing the hundredfold return. It's about Him staying true to us even when we aren't perfect. He has proven all of His principles to me in spite of my imperfections. He knows we still love Him, and He certainly loves us. He considers the motive of the heart; it's about the most awesome way to live that one could imagine—with God Himself as your friend. If you slip, get up, and keep going, you will see that He didn't quit on you. You are still His child and are still under His grace. He loves you fervently!

He is strong and wise and wonderful. I am weak and foolish and ordinary. When I was nearly stricken to death with loneliness, pain of loss, and grief, He showed me the way out, and it was out and beyond myself, toward a spirit of caring and giving. It works every time. He also added in joy and laughter. What He does for one, He'll do for all. You do have a say-so in your future, your attitude, your success, and your happiness, as well as the way you handle (and survive) the difficult times in your life. This is your life, and you only get one time around. Caring about others and giving for their sake gets you out of yourself. Make faith and love choices. Do you want to stand with God or without God, trust Him or not trust Him, live by faith or live by fear? Your future success is controlled by the choices you make.

"[What, what would have become of me] had I not believed to see the Lord's goodness in the land of the living! Wait and hope for and expect the Lord; be brave and of good courage, and let your heart be stout and enduring. Yes, wait and hope for and expect the Lord" (Ps. 27:13–14, Amp).

During our earlier years in Tennessee, around 1991, we needed some timber thinned out. An acquaintance of ours recommended a man for the job and said he was an honest timber cutter who was a good man and who would never steal logs from landowners, as he had said that many did. I had already talked to two others and had not made a decision, so I said the man could come see what we needed to have done and then give us a price. He made a better offer than the other two, and we made the deal. The two owners of that small timber operation were brothers, Roger (better known as Rodg) and Ronnie Matlock. This is how I came to meet Rodg—and then, years later, to marry him.

Because Rodg came into our lives near the time when Greg had arrived from Maryland, he slowly became a friend to our entire family, and we had a few years to get to know each other on that basis. He had been married, but he had become divorced several years prior to our meeting. That made it possible for him to live near his new job with us so he had moved a small motor home to a tract of land on our property beside the river. Mr. Ralph had recently had quintuple bypass surgery, and his memory was not normal. Scottie was very ill, and Greg had mistakenly (according to Rodg's way of thinking) moved there with the idea of fishing during his recreational time. Rodg immediately undertook introducing him to the wonderful world (according to them) of arrowhead and Civil War relic hunting. They eventually had enough river stories to fill a book, which would sound similar to stories told about Tom Sawyer and Huckleberry Finn. He provided a place of normalcy and friendship in each of their lives, for which I will be eternally grateful.

Whenever I briefly contemplated life after Mr. Ralph, it was settled in my heart that I would never marry again. Besides, I honestly thought that he would be healed. I also knew in my heart that I would never want to have to get to know another person with the idea of marrying him. I had heard a preacher say, "If you are thinking about getting married to someone, the *real person* is hiding in a closet somewhere." It was humorously intended to inspire us to really get to know a person before taking that step. Because our friendship with Rodg originated as a long-term business arrangement, we came to know one another as being just who we were, with the frankness that casual friends reveal about themselves, their character, and their attitudes, and with neither of us trying to impress the other, nor offer false pretenses.

By 1994, our family was at one of the lowest of times with the illnesses of my husband and my son. This part is made brief, but believe me, living it seemed unending at times. There were nightmare situations that will be left untold. There were reasons for the fear that my family felt regarding my safety, coming out of the Alzheimer's grip on our family. I never believed that Mr. Ralph would hurt me—someone else, maybe, but not me. I was frightened a few times, but he never did really hurt me. I loved him so much that I had to take care of him myself. I tried to hire outside help to come to our home a few times, but the distance and remote location of our home was a problem, and the nature of the illness was also a problem. One man who tried to help me said that he would never try that again; Mr. Ralph had scared him by threatening him. One of Mr. Ralph's sons had a similar experience when he came to visit his dad from Virginia.

It was so important for me to stay in faith, believing, hopeful, cheerful, positive, and encouraging to all the other members of my family. For the most part, I did—but, deep inside the intense feelings of loneliness cried out, "I am the wife, I am the mother; why do I have to be the strong one? Who comforts me?" Whether we like it or not, the human side of us is not always all that easy to control, and the grief and pain that I felt cried out to be expressed. I managed fairly well, but it was only controlled—not gone.

There came a time when the agony and pressure of trying to attend to Mr. Ralph's needs were overlapping into the final days of Scottie's life. Scottie had been partly comatose, sometimes in and out of awareness and barely speaking in a whisper, if at all. I had been sleeping on a mattress from our camper in the floor of Scottie's room. Because there were terrible strangling sounds that would regularly come from his throat, I had been instructed in how to use the respirator to give him temporary relief. Most people cannot imagine my pain as a loving mother in fulfilling the necessity of that procedure; it was nearly unbearable. He never struggled or resisted. At the same time I was also the loving wife of a precious man who was getting worse all the time, not better as I had prayed for and expected.

Mr. Ralph had lost all reasoning by then and was extremely jealous and emotionally threatened by the other sick person I was trying to keep alive through faith, knowing that "in the natural" both diseases were terminal at that time. One night I had been laying across the end of Scottie's bed, talking to him. Mr. Ralph actually pulled me off the end of Scottie's bed and dragged me down the hall to our room. I closed the door so that Scottie could not hear our voices. Please understand that reasoning was not an option; praying or quoting scriptures continued, but Mr. Ralph's behavior did not seem to improve. Certainly I had hoped that the prayers would have a spiritual effect, but we were mostly drawn into the "beg, cajole, or demand" stage of Mr. Ralph's disease in attempting to maintain some semblance of control. He definitely had periods of calm behavior at times, but there was no way to predict that from moment to moment. During that particular episode, I had finally convinced him to allow me to leave the room. When I opened the door, Scottie, who had no physical strength left at all, had managed to get off his bed and pull himself down a long hallway then across the floor of another room. It was a long distance. He had made it to just outside our door. I asked him what on earth he was doing, and he answered, "Mom, I had to try to help you. I thought he was going to hurt you." Needless to say, that compounded the heartbreak and distress concerning both of them. I understood the principle of using God's Word to get rid of sickness and disease, and I was trying to stand firmly on the Word. I requested prayer from some of the large ministries that I love and trust. I was not attempting to do it alone as the most *comfortable* and *natural* position to me had always seemed to be *second* in command. Pride was not an issue.

At that point Mr. Ralph, (and for a brief moment it occurred to me to use the word "Alzheimer's" instead of "Mr. Ralph" for his name because that person was not the Mr. Ralph that any of us knew) carried a threat of physical strength that could be used against others, sometimes had no patience at all, and was in constant need of attention also, because of his illness. In his healthy, normal mind, he was as kind and dear as a person could ever be. I want to emphasize that I tell this with great respect toward him. It is necessary to touch on it though, in order to honestly describe some of the terribleness of that disease generated

from the devil, and the situation—for all of us. If I stayed in Scottie's room too long, I wouldn't know where Mr. Ralph was or what he was doing, which could be anywhere or anything. He needed full-time attention regarding activities, needs, meals, baths, and being quieted or comforted. But Scottie also needed constant vigilance. Greg had his hands full with an unhappy wife, three children (two were hers and one they had together), and the obligation to earn a living. He helped me as much as he could, as he loved both Scottie and Mr. Ralph very much.

The Alzheimer's was at a stage where Mr. Ralph was restless and unsettled. I am sure that in spite of it all, he sensed that terrible things were happening to our family. He wouldn't go to bed at night and stay there, unless I lay down with him until he went to sleep. During that time I felt pressure to care for him but to also be at my son's side. The desperation of the situation was heartbreaking, suffocating, nerve-racking, and exhausting. Scottie's nurse, Marsha, came regularly but could never stay very long. My sleep was only in naps between their needs. I guess my faith was trying to interrupt the destiny of these two men without my realizing it, but I did know that the faith I had didn't seem to be changing the situation in the way that I hoped. Sometimes I wondered if a stronger Christian would be more effective, and I feel certain that there are Christians who believe that they could have changed it with their faith. Believe me, there will be days when the strongest of the strong will be made to remember that God is the only one who never fails. There have been plenty of times in my life when things would be going well for me while someone else had been in a terrible struggle. I have occasionally wondered after hearing about a death, whether or not my faith might have been more effective in the case of whoever was praying, when theirs didn't seem to have been. If I know that the praying people are faith-filled Christians, I don't wonder about that any more, and I apologize for ever having done so. It is good to have confidence in your faith, while maintaining humility. Only God knows these answers anyway. I lived with a heavy feeling of responsibility to be able to help them be set free through my faith and prayers. Maybe it was also just meant to be.

I can still tell you from my heart that I did not doubt God. Myself, yes, but never God. In spite of all of the pain and loss, I was the only one subjected to criticism in my heart. I did not maintain well or to my own satisfaction. I remember how often, before Mr. Ralph and Scottie had gotten so far into their illnesses that I would plead with them to believe with me and to stand strong in faith in their own behalf. It's impossible to know another person's thinking, but often I have found that people do not spiritually receive the idea of being healed by faith for themselves. We can believe it for others easier than we can for ourselves; we are too conditioned to believe in modern medicine so that much of our hope lies in doctors and medication. For me, if it was a test of faith for their healing, I thought I had failed. But in offering a ray of hope regarding your personal responsibility toward the healing of anyone in a similar situation, if the sick person is a Christian and is still in a responsible state of mind, perhaps he or she has some responsibility too, at least in not believing *against your faith* by thinking that for some reason it's not going to work for them. They need to put their faith into operation too, if they are able minded.

Take into consideration the enthusiasm that has been prevalent in my attitude about God throughout this book. Because I stayed determined to keep God as the essence and the very necessity of my life, He remained with me. He knew that I felt so brokenhearted. He knew what we all need to remember: we are human beings with frailties and weaknesses. He helps us when we cannot help ourselves. He turns bad situations into living testimonies. He is God, and we need Him and the tender care He gives us. We cannot recover and continue to serve Him with zeal and enthusiasm if we do not trust His love for us. His blood was shed for us so that we could be made whole and healthy again, both spiritually and physically.

One afternoon during this terrible and most trying and time, Scottie seemed to be resting peacefully, and Mr. Ralph was outside with Rodg, who had taken a break from his work to check on us. The sun and the idea of fresh air seemed so appealing that I decided that I could leave Scott for just a few minutes. I had sat down on a tree stump, even mourning the loss of that particular tree. Mr. Ralph had told Rodg to cut it along with three others without my knowledge, and at that particular time Rodg had not been around long enough to realize that Mr. Ralph didn't know which trees to cut or to leave. I had been remiss in not explaining to Rodg the details of our personal situation prior to that, and so the memory of when I discovered that those big oaks had been cut truly did add to my sadness and feelings of frustration and loss.

Anyway, on this day I was being grateful for the fresh, clean air. I remember looking at Rodg and thinking how healthy and fit and calm he was, and I was trying to remember when life had been healthy and fit and normal for my family. It was good to have Rodg for a friend because he was always offering to help us however he could. He felt most comfortable talking about manly things like cars, equipment, the woods, and the river. Scottie's vast knowledge about almost anything was interesting to him. Rodg was Mr. Ralph's favorite person besides me. Rodg was always bringing him interesting little stones and arrowheads from the river, and Mr. Ralph needed a friend. Rodg and Greg were good friends too, and I was so thankful for that. Greg had moved his family from Maryland to Tennessee in order to be with his brother for as long as possible, and he needed a friend. Rodg had started the timber job at about the same time that Greg had moved there, and he had taught Greg the ropes, as the river and our Tennessee wilderness were new to Greg. As for Scottie, when he had still been able to sit up and talk, Rodg would just go in and visit with him for a while from time to time because he liked Scottie and wanted to be kind. Scott was very fond of him and had told me that he thought Rodg was a really good man. The men had it made with camaraderie among them, but my role with each of them carried responsible guidelines. The boundaries of the titles and expectations of wife, mother, or business associate put me in a different role. I did a lot of praying, cooking, nursing, cleaning, grocery shopping, and being responsible for many duties. I almost never went on the river; I didn't really have time to do much else except to rest at any opportunity that I had. Rodg had told me later that we were the only family that he had ever been around that said "I love you" to each other, which we did at every opportunity. He became the best friend our family ever had because he saw the enormity and seriousness of the devastation that we appeared to be heading toward—like watching a car stalled on the railroad track with a speeding train rumbling round the bend.

By that point, I felt like my thoughts were drowning in what I knew the future held, unless a miracle occurred. I totally believed that a miracle could still occur, but the Alzheimer's had been gaining ground for seven years at that point, and Scottie had been becoming more seriously ill over the past three years. I could not even consider the thought of Scottie and Mr. Ralph both leaving me, yet it inevitably would come to my mind. I had assumed that when the timber job was finished, Rodg would just move back to Ramer, Tennessee, fifty-five miles away, and go on with his life. I also thought that he and Greg would take an occasional arrowhead hunting trip and remain pals. But I was wondering if two of the men in the family who were Rodg's friends did actually die, would he still think of me as a friend too, so I asked him that question. His response was that he would. I breathed in the fresh April air a little longer and then returned to Scottie's room. From that time on I too knew that I had a friend for life.

Scottie went to glory about two weeks after that. I continued to live on the river, still surrounded by woods and wilderness, and Greg built several houses on the property. His wife took her two children that she had had when Greg married her, and went back to Maryland; Greg was awarded custody of their daughter, Rebecca. Mr. Ralph's condition had worsened and gone into different, deeper stages. The only activity that would keep him settled and comfortable was to watch the Gaither Family music videos, or to have Rodg visit him. I continued to pray for his healing and to love him very much. In July 1999 he went to glory, dying peacefully from pneumonia. At the time that he died, our family doctor, who had then been our doctor for ten years, had warned me about my health too. I was overweight, depressed, and exhausted from lack of rest and sleep. I had plantar fasciitis in both feet, and so I could not lie down allowing my heels to touch the bed. Standing up in the mornings (or the middle of the night) produced terrible pain. Actually, I neither wanted to get up or face another day of our torment. I could, only because and in spite of everything, I still expected my Jesus to be with us, and He was. I felt abject failure because I thought that I had failed everybody in one way or another. But I could not let go of God or fail to believe that He had been and was still with all of us, including me. I knew the character of each member of our little group, and I knew the character of Jesus. I learned through a really difficult way that if you stand by Jesus, He will stand by you. In the midst of your toughest test, you can find yourself in both failure and victory, but the real test and the real victory comes when you keep trying and keep holding on to Jesus, no matter what. Referencing 2 Timothy 2:9 (Amp), I have suffered affliction and even worn spiritual chains, "But the Word of God is not chained or imprisoned!" It is our lifeline, and to keep trusting Him and *trying* to live by the Gospel is the true purpose of our life.

I had gone through the fire, so to speak, and had suffered both trials and failures. Through the cleansing power of the risen Christ, He humbled, taught, corrected, and provided me with whatever was necessary for my future well-being and to see that I followed His purpose for my life, as that was my prayer. He continues to allow the trials of life to bring us closer to Him – not push us farther away from Him, as Satan's intent is. I have received further training in the righteousness (or right-standing) of Christ. I truly praise Him for that. When Rodg and I were later pronounced man and wife by a pastor friend, he had witnessed many years of hardship and pain in my family. No one was over the heart-breaking losses that we had suffered, and we never would be, humanly speaking. But, humanly speaking, we also needed to accept that Scottie and Mr. Ralph were now joyfully in Heaven, and we needed to work on repairing and resubmitting any areas that could or would keep us from ordering our lives aright. Our attention needed to be focused on following His instructions toward restoration, both spiritually and physically.

We knew that Mr. Ralph and Scottie would have appreciated that they were now in Heaven, that we would always love them dearly, and would be joining them when our time came. None of us believed in the death-threatening grip of the spirit of grief, especially when it is attempting to pull someone completely under. Our new path was to accept His guidance in moving forward, still striving to be victorious through hope in His Word, mercy, and grace. II Cor. 4:1, 5 (NKJV) "Therefore, since we have this ministry, as we have received mercy, we do not lose heart." Verse 5 says "For we do not preach ourselves, but Christ Jesus the Lord, and ourselves as your bondservants for Jesus' sake." Our little family had been devastatingly fractured. We picked up the pieces of what remained, regained our spiritual footing, regrouped, and proceeded on with life on this earth. Rodg and I went from being good friends to being married good friends.

Here are a few scriptures that can bless us all if we receive them as from Him. They are in James 4–5 (Amp). James 4 tells us to draw near to God, to humble ourselves, to feel very insignificant in His presence, and He will exalt us. He will lift us up and make our lives significant. Verse 11 says not to speak evil about or accuse one another; we are not to malign or judge a Christian brother or sister. Chapter 5 says that we are not to complain against one another, so that we ourselves may not be judged. Verse 11 says, "You know how we call those blessed (happy) who were steadfast—who endured. You have heard of the endurance of Job; and you have seen the Lord's [purpose and how He richly blessed him in the] end, in as much as the Lord is full of pity and compassion and tenderness and mercy."

> ***The Spirit Filled Life Bible*** offers a note on James 1:2–5: "**The testing of faith produces patience (the ability to endure), which is the hallmark of the mature believer. Only under the pressure of trials can the believer test the true depth of his faith in God. The established heart will not waver, but will rejoice in the knowledge of the goodness of God.**"

When I read James 1:2–4 (Amp), it is a very reassuring scripture because it says that when we are enveloped in or encounter trials of any sort, or when we fall into various temptations, the trial and proving of our faith bring out endurance and steadfastness and patience. We should allow them to have full play and do a thorough work.

Because we cannot purify ourselves, submitting ourselves to be purified by God is necessary for believers. His holiness shows through when sin is dethroned. That implies to me that we may make some incorrect responses during the process, especially if the test is severe. It is also clear that because of God's pity, compassion, tenderness, and mercy (James 5:11, Amp), He knows the true heart of every person and whether we welcome and receive the Word with a humble, gentle spirit, wanting it implanted and rooted in our heart. If we are truly striving to be obedient and respectful to Him, then being subjected to a thorough work to make us be more "holy, as He is holy" (Lev. 11:45) should be appreciated for what it is. The trial and the testing achieve the bringing out, proving, having full play to do a thorough work, so that we can be perfectly and fully developed, which sounds like a refining process: a negative element will likely appear, but it is then disposed of—thus, being refined. God loves and forgives, and we learn and try again because we love Him too. I yearn to have the nature of Christ and to live for God. It's an uphill climb, but look at who and what waits at the top!

About a year after Mr. Ralph died, Greg and I sold all of our river property and moved to a lake community still in Tennessee but not far from where our rural homes had been. Rodg's livelihood keeps him stationed in Ramer most of the week, but all of his weekends are spent with me and our three little rescued doggies. Greg is remarried to Brandy, and she has two precious children, Shelby and Jacob, plus they have Tylan Grace together. Rebecca is grown and has a baby girl named Moriahjo; they live in Maryland and are both beautiful, precious girls. We love them so very much.

In 2003, Rodg and I had built a smaller version of a plantation house on a forty-acre farm in Ramer. We had alpacas for a while, and they truly are adorable creatures. From that we developed a business selling alpaca products, primarily the wonderful socks made from their fleece. That decision was very successful and proved to be a great retirement hobby, but a turn of fate changed our direction again in 2007. In 2008 the farm was sold, and I moved a few miles from Jackson, Tennessee. My mother is now in serious medical condition and I visit her every day. Because of his job, Rodg was always gone by 5:00 a.m. every day and sometimes not at home again until almost bedtime which left me with a lot of free time. I was also fifty miles away from family needs that I could have been helping with. Because there were health issues in both our families, we made a family decision about how we could do the most good for our families, so he is still in Ramer, where he and his brother have their business and their shop for working on large logging equipment. The house that Rodg had lived in when we married is on the same property as their shop, and he stays there during the work week. Their mother lives alone in Ramer, does not drive, and he regularly assists her. So for now, this is our life—and we are fine with it, are fulfilling different responsibilities, and are spending great quality time with each other on weekends and during times off work for Rodg. Greg is an excellent builder and has built the home that I live in today. It is the sixth house that I have had built since the move to Tennessee. I have lived in five of them and have no regrets. This has been my particular life. Any house that I have had to leave (for sound reasons each time, which have all proven to be productive in ministry, one way or another) has been a wonderful memory, and this last one will hold the blessing of completing *Come Walk With Me To Glory*. Being bored or looking back is not a condition that I have. Sometimes that requires my *will*, but my *will* is to stay active in the Kingdom of God and to move wherever He sends me. Thank You, God, for that!

Because of God and my love for Him, I honestly have a joyful heart. Ever since I became a spirit-filled Christian, my heart has been dedicated to God, even during the very worst and lowest of times, as well as in the high places. I wouldn't be here today if not for Him, and I wouldn't have kept joy in my heart, which gave me strength and hope to not give up when things were at rock bottom. I found that being at rock bottom has you firmly on the rock of ages, if you choose to trust Him.

Rodg and Dian - 2003

And now, so that you know something more about what my new life is like, let me tell you a couple of things about Rodg, so that by knowing him better, you will also know that I am being blessed beyond measure. Rodg, Greg and his family, and writing this book to fulfill a part of God's purpose for my life—all have provided the perfect existence for me. We have little reminders of Mr. Ralph and Scottie around the house, and they are definitely in our hearts. Rodg and I have been married for several years now and we are still good friends. We attend church on Sunday with Greg, Brandy, and the three children.

Rodg actually received an invitation some time ago to accompany a professional team on an archeological dig in search of the Ark of the Covenant. The distance and time away from home was more than he was willing to sacrifice. He is the only person I have personally known who claims finding the Ark as his greatest dream this side of Heaven.

In providing a little bit of background information about Rodg, he honestly believes that he is a cousin to Mike Huckabee, because his mother's maiden name was Huckabee before she married, and she was from McNairy County, Tennessee. He has some very old cherry trees that are supposed to have come from Brother Mike's family about one hundred years ago. Rodg is not looking for the limelight and has never confirmed this information. He does, however, call Brother Mike "Cuz" whenever he sees him on TV. In either case, Rodg is a fan of Brother Mike, and so am I.

Another "claim to fame" was that an old acquaintance of Rodg's talked him into going into the army as a teenager—and to stop running bootleg whiskey, which would have ended his life sooner rather than later in those days. Rodg's life in that time and place was very representative of making, selling, and running moonshine as a way of life. He was under the false impression that it was his only choice for income and survival. He accepted the sound advice of the man who persuaded him differently, and we will always be grateful to the famous Sheriff Buford Pusser for his act of wisdom in convincing Rodg to join the army and to give up the way of life that he had inherited.

The US Army and Vietnam placed Rodg in an unimaginably different world. He transitioned quickly from a courageous, adventurous boy often on the wrong side of the law to a very courageous, adventurous man on the right side of everything. After his return home, his reputation became centered on his character instead of his past, which I think we could all appreciate. Even to this day, people seek out Rodg when they need help with anything. He's just that kind of man—"country" in the best possible respect, kind and quiet with great inner strength. He never seeks praise; he just does the right thing, and that's his way of thinking on how it should be done.

I really admire the peaceful, honest, down-to-earth man that he is. It has been hard for him to change sometimes, because that inner toughness can work against a person too. When he told me of his salvation experience, he said that even though God was urging him to go down to the altar, he was gripping the back of the pew in front of him, trying so hard not to go that his knuckles turned very white. I can just see those blue-gray eyes in that handsome face set like flint in firm determination. Thank God, he finally gave up, and God won. I expect it was quite a tussle, but now he holds just as firmly to God's way. He is so well liked by everyone who meets him, and he never tries to be anything but Rodg, and he's really good at it!

I often speak with respect and admiration for my late husband, who taught me about truly becoming a new person in Christ Jesus. Rodg doesn't feel the least bit threatened about that part of my life, and I am not threatened by his past. Like we've heard said, it's what we've done and where we've been that makes us who we are today. That was then, this is now, and we live for each other with our focus on God and Heaven. He is a good friend and a great blessing, and he has kept me steady on the course of life, time after time, including and during the most difficult trials of my life.

We were married late in life, and I lovingly refer to him as my "snow in the pines man." The picture that comes immediately to my mind is a peaceful, quiet setting of the beauty and weightiness of an expanse of heavy snow settling on tall, green pines. They are laden with the snowy weight on the boughs, pulling them down as they stand in silent peace. Yet that melting snow turns out to be a blessing to the earth, although the trees didn't understand their burden at the time. Still, they carried it with patient endurance, displaying it magnificently and then loyally lifting their branches back toward the sun when the snow was gone. That's my Rodg and my life with him. Sounds like a life well lived, doesn't it?

A little bit of age, a lot of life, and the wisdom we've found in each other and in God gives us a synchronized walk of contentment and love. We're happy with today because we absolutely know it's in God's hands, and we're ready for tomorrow because we know He's on our side. It is a win-win situation, and however mismatched we may sometimes seem to the world around us, we are very happy. We think we have a near-perfect marriage.

I have stated that I never doubted God, but just for the record, I also never blamed my precious Lord for any of my difficulties, as people so often do. If He allowed them, He had a reason. It's not about me; it's about Him and what He is working out for mankind. I do not question God. Trials happen in our lives, and we can persevere and respond with trust in Him, or we can throw in the towel. My faith was not always up to par, but my trust in God never wavered. Faith and trust are two different things. Faith requires my action toward depending on God and His Word. Trust involves only God because of whom He is. Without Him there would have been no hope. I always looked to Him for the way out, and He always brought me through, each time with blessings heaped upon blessings. The losses remain tremendous, but I have been able to see part of God's overall plan regarding our family in the time since then, because I have seen ministry, miracles, salvation, and blessings blossom in the wake of those losses. I know for a fact that much has been accomplished through victories obtained because of our trials and how we responded to them. It is solely because of Him that my life has been so extraordinary. He has blessed and guided me through what sometimes feels like six normal lifetimes. He has given me two unbelievable sons, two great loves, a heart devoted to His cause, and now a lovely home that *this* time I really intend to stay put in ... but who knows; never say never. Rodg says he will retire soon and then be here with us full-time. I have to say that I would really be surprised at that, because he is not a stay-indoors man. Nothing is set in concrete when you are willing to follow and trust God.

Sometimes, because we know that we live a different life than the "usual," we laughingly remark that though others are worrying about us because Rodg's work requires him to live elsewhere during the weekdays, we are not only happy, but we are being productive in ways important to our well-being and to that of others. God doesn't use a cookie cutter on people, and no two are alike—and isn't that grand! I am so blessed and grateful that He gave me such a unique, interesting, easygoing, and independent man who loves me. Thank You, God, and thank you, Rodg.

God bless you, and I love you,
Dian

Chapter Ten

Thoughts on a Sunday Afternoon

During a Sunday school class at House of Mercy Church in Morris Chapel, Tennessee, as always the opportunity was given to make prayer requests. Nobody ever said that they didn't have one—we all did, all the time.

Later, during the morning service, Pastor Dennis Moffett had challenged the congregation to consider that the spirit of God was actually in the sanctuary with us. When we were invited to praise Him, very little changed in the room, even though we all loved the Lord. He encouraged us again, saying, "If God walked down the center aisle, what would you do?" This was a serious question to the church—what would we do? The pastor would be pleased to know that one sermon triggered this much contemplation during the drive home from church on a Sunday afternoon.

In many services in my life, I have been amazed at what effect religion and tradition have had on people not being willing to show enthusiasm for our one and only magnificent God. Tapping your foot or smiling seems a bit condescending, don't you think? We can do that without even intending to. However, if you open up your heart and actually sense and feel the presence of God there with you, stirring down in your soul, why doesn't that move you—literally? Don't you *want* to show your joy? How could we be confronted with the presence of God and not show it? Is it that we aren't aware or are we too timid to participate? We are confronted with His presence in our church, every time we come here.

Certainly church is a place for reverence and order and respect, but the Bible also says that He inhabits the praises of His people, and a joyful "praise and worship" time is good for us and blesses God's heart. Ask King David, or read the Psalms if you think that God doesn't welcome a display of excitement in His behalf. He enjoyed it then and would now; He hasn't changed—only we have changed.

This is not a request for people to go against their normal ways of showing excitement or enthusiasm. It is just asking folks to be willing to do as much for God as they do for their human heroes. Do what you feel in your heart toward Him in recognition of being in His extraordinary presence. Why shouldn't you say, "Thank You, Jesus," and lift your hands toward Him in love, if you feel that acknowledging Him would be showing an act of love? We should want to encourage His presence to be with us in even greater measure. When a vision of the Shekinah glory of the Lord filled the temple, "the posts of the door moved at the voice of him that cried, and the house was filled with smoke" (Isa. 6:1–8). Are we ready for that, are we pleading for that, or have we not thought much about needing that kind of presence?

Can you agree with me on this? "Yes, Lord, I am ready, pleading, and needing this powerful manifestation of Your glory in our presence. I will declare right now that if God will show us the opportunity to have His presence here in that measure, so that the doorposts shake and the temple fills with smoke, we will stay put and not bolt, acknowledge Him in outstanding praise, and fall prostrate at His feet in love, respect, and honor to His glorious name!"

Now, with that notion and prayer being pictured in our soul, let's analyze our present behavior and attitude toward prayer and praise. We'll get back to our thrilling hope shortly.

What do you do when you are watching a game with the score tied in the last minute, and your favorite team is near a championship win? Or when your eight-year-old is on third base in the Little League game? What about when you found out you were having a baby or got your first home? These are all exciting things of the world. God gives us every good thing we have; He's the source of those times of blessing and joy, and of our life and breath—and we do love Him, don't we? Because of His goodness and love, we should lift Him up with our praise, begging for more of His glorious manifestation. Let Him see the hunger in our soul for His holy presence; let Him know that He's not only welcome but longed for!

Don't just praise Him—that's an elementary step. Cry out for Him and seek His glory. Why do we stop short? If it's because we're "satisfied," then we need to get unsatisfied again. This does not mean being unpleased or ungrateful for what He gives us. This is not about what He gives us at all, but about how we are inclined to accept worldly blessings as His sign of favor toward us. He doesn't want us to be like two-year-olds who get totally involved with their gifts. We should be grateful for everything He gives and does, but we should not stop in our pursuit of holiness because we feel blessed and satisfied.

> **If we want more of the powerful, miracle-working favor of God, we need to press on, press against, press for, and press again. If our goal is to see the glory of God, then we can't be satisfied with simple pleasures. We're allowing ourselves to be bought off if things of this world can so easily distract us from deep yearning and constant striving.**

For instance, one gift from God could be that you become motivated and are allowed to lead someone to Jesus, or to have a spirit that longs for God so strongly that He will manifest Himself before your church. Those gifts would really be worth yearning for. Have we been praying for that sort of favor from God, or are we saturated and satisfied by worldly desires? Remember, we really and truly want to see this sanctuary filled with His Shekinah glory, so we have to figure out what exactly could get Him here to that degree—a praising, yearning, "crying out for Him" bunch of people, or a people that are "quite satisfied"?

When you're in a happy, worldly mode—say at a birthday party—nobody cares if you have paint on your face, put feathers in your hair, or put on a clown suit; you just think you're having fun, and you're all in it together. But take the same group of people and put them in church, if you can get them there at all, and they refuse to move. Some may even shudder at the idea, but not in the spirit. Have you noticed that fear is one reason we don't want to participate by physically demonstrating our love? We think our dignity will be compromised. Remember who that spirit of fear comes from? "For God has not given us a spirit of fear, but of *power and of love and of a sound mind*" (2 Tim. 1:7, emphasis added). The *Amplified Bible* refers to the spirit of fear as "timidity, cowardice, craven, cringing, and fawning." That actually describes what my first feelings were when going from another denomination into a "full Gospel" church. Well, fear is false evidence appearing real, and it makes people believe that if they show signs of rejoicing with praises for God, it will somehow diminish their appearance of being well-mannered and dignified. If people think that way about you, they need prayer because they don't really know the Word. Contrast choosing the idea of giving up your dignity with the idea of keeping your fear. The previous one brings the glory of God, whereas the other brings false evidence from you-know-where.

Dignity, according to *Merriam-Webster's Dictionary*, means "the quality or state of being worthy, honored, or esteemed." We try to protect our personal dignity. Whose eyes are you really trying to please through praise, though? Why not give up cowardice and become a brave heart, even praying that those other people that you were concerned about will decide to do the same? We wouldn't even exist without Him forming us with His own hands and then breathing life into us. We were equivalent to mud pies at one point in time, but thanks to Him we can now walk and talk—and praise Him for what He has done for us. Or do you want to use those precious, God-given abilities only for human achievement? Other people need encouragement too, need to see someone step out, forget self, and set an example of love for God rather than self. Recognition and honor toward God is so pleasing and respectful to Him, and even though we can't see Him visibly, He sees us. We can't see the wind either, but we feel it and know it's there. If you want God to have a gift back, then praise Him in the sanctuary (and everywhere else, for that matter). Go so far as to look at it like this: In giving up your dignity, you are offering a sacrifice of praise; a sacrifice is something one would prefer to keep but is willing to give up. Don't you enjoy the idea of having a personal offering to place on that altar for Him? It might just get our doorposts shaking, and wouldn't that be grand! Remember, that's what our *aim* is!

It is important to recognize these most common diversions that pull us away from worshipping with a (Godly) spiritual attitude—and then discard the diversions once and for all. If you identify with this negative reaction (which is common among mankind), let yourself hear, understand, and resist it from this point on, being set free by the power of the truth of God's Word. You will totally enjoy the freedom to worship, once you are free from the (previous) "dignity spirit" and have broken those chains that bound you. Thank you, Father, for the freedom that Your love brings.

Lifting holy hands unto the Lord as the Bible instructs us to do (1 Tim. 2:8) is an act of surrender. If someone puts a gun in your back, wouldn't you say, "I surrender"? Well, there's no gun with God, just your freewill choice on whether you look grateful, pliable, and loveable toward Him. Do you surrender all, or just enough to barely get by? If we can't get past our self-absorption enough to trust Him in worship, how can we be useful in our testimony? If it takes nerve to praise Him in gratitude for His goodness—even among Christians, with Him being our Father who loves us–how then can we face the unknown of a stranger, hoping to convince him or her about the Gospel? So what are we asking *from* God, anyway—just life, breath, and health? He provides all that and more, so what is His worth to us, and aren't we glad that He didn't concern Himself with dignity when He was spit on, stripped of His clothes, and hung before all on that cross, watching His own blood run down in a crimson flow for you and me? Think about this please: What is His *worth* to you? Is He not worth your dignity and your submission? Well then, let's shake off those slack and drooping hands, and let them serve their true purpose to praise God and demonstrate to others that we believe that He is real and that we have a willing heart to serve Him (Heb. 12:12–14, Amp). Actions do speak louder than words, you know.

We have the personal choice to overcome that stubborn or fearful spirit with our will, if we choose to. Our worth, our honor, and our self-esteem come from God. He can give us more of all of those in a healthy balance, not based in fear but in His power and love. We should listen to the right voice, as Isaiah 12:5–6 (Amp) states: "Sing praises to the Lord, for He has done excellent things—gloriously; let this be made known in all the earth. Cry aloud and shout joyfully, you women and inhabitants of Zion, for great in your midst is the Holy One of Israel." Glory to God!

All of these thoughts about people's difficulty in responding to God in a way that was pleasing to Him, and not themselves, were going through my mind, as well as remembering the different prayer requests that had been made in Sunday school. As I went over each one, asking God to help my sweet sisters, I realized how unemotional my prayers sounded—like the worship portion of the church service had started out. In analyzing that thought, I wondered if prayers even count if we don't really have our heart in them. Our minds and our hopes may be sincere, but what about compassion stirring behind those prayers, giving them a force of love, pushing them on and up?

A "Fish" Story—but True

Then the strangest thing happened. As I drove along a quiet country highway toward home, with no lakes, ponds, or streams in sight, I saw a fish lying in the middle of the road. It was almost unbelievable, and I wondered whether I was really seeing a fish. I realized that it was real—and it was still alive. Its tail went up and down, and it bowed its body in desperation. This is not a pleasant story, but I want to tell it the way it unfolded to me. It bowed its body away from the extremely hot pavement. So many thoughts went through my mind; I had no way to save it because I had neither container nor water. The only human explanation for how it got there was that it had been in the back of a pickup and had jumped or sloshed out of a fisherman's bucket. I guess because fish are cold-blooded and not cute like a puppy, people have very little compassion for them. This fish was different; he was breaking my heart.

I understood that it was in a life struggle, and for some reason I thought that instinctively it knew that water was nowhere near. It was in the middle of a highway, and it was gasping for its source of oxygen. Its skin was drying and burning from the sun, and one of its eyes was being seared by the hot pavement. It was a scene of total despair and hopelessness, with no help on the way. I felt so much compassion and sadness for that fish. I can only think that I felt so much for it because I was watching it have to lie there without hope, with it sensing (in my imagination, at least) that it could not live or swim again. I felt desperate and even sadder because I was its only apparent answer, and there was absolutely nothing I could do.

As is my usual way, I contemplated the sad event and wondered what was to be learned from God by my having to watch a creature's death struggle, feeling so sad. Then I knew. There were two parts.

First, people who are lost are living without hope, and we are their only answer. The heat and lack of water is torture. The people can't take the heat, and they do require the living water of the Word to survive. The poor fish only knew the present; the lost know nothing of the eternal future. Don't think you're at the end of your rope, and do have compassion for whoever you might meet along the roadway of life. Don't lie there in abandonment, and don't allow anyone else to. Call on the God of power and answers, for those who trust and ask of Him. Don't create or ignore a spiritual scene; study and dwell on unusual things that happen, just to see if there might not be a teaching in it, as sometimes there really are modern-day parables.

Our positive praise and our heartfelt prayers bring the power for our personal testimony. Hebrews 11:1 says that faith is the "title deed" to what you have not yet seen. This is a message of hope to share. Faith does perceive as real fact what is not yet revealed to the senses. Share the message of faith to help folks get out of their hopeless situations. Did salvation not assure you of your title deed to Heaven? Faith and salvation are both spiritual laws from God. Don't you believe He'll deliver both title deeds to you, and to the lost? Of course you do! Share it.

Second, long ago, during a time of terrible persecution of Christians, the sign of a fish was drawn on the doorpost of homes to secretly identify that the home was occupied by fellow Christians, and one could find shelter or safety there. The message to me in this was that Christians (represented by the sign of the fish) should have compassion (which I was now feeling) when they pray. I got it right away. I remembered that the *Amplified Bible* says in James 5:16, "heartfelt, fervent prayer avails much." My prayers were being, I am ashamed to say, sincere but not fervent.

I decided to try an experiment to push my spirit's involvement with my faith, and to hope for some greater degree of success in my prayers. I made myself feel the compassion again that I had felt moments before. With that stirring of compassion in my soul, I prayed again, no longer thinking of the poor fish but transferring that feeling within me to the needs of others. Once I began to pray with the stirring in my spirit, it was easy to continue to feel it for another's needs. I realized that sometimes prayer requests inspire concern but may not provide enough of a picture in our mind to get hold of our compassion to the effective level of a prayer. Often there are very few details given because the request is personal, which is fine—it's just that our mental image doesn't provide a picture and often doesn't sense the seriousness of the request. The key that has come to me is this: we need to be sure that we involve our hearts when we pray. Having compassion made the prayer feel different and real; it made me feel that I had offered up a real prayer that God would hear. It was real compassion and used for the right purpose, just acquired in a roundabout way, through an object lesson. God allowed me to understand the lesson.

I had never thought of borrowed compassion before, but sometimes we need a jump-start. I will ask the Holy Spirit to help me pray as I ought (Rom. 8:26–27), because He makes intercession for us, and He who searches our hearts knows what the mind of the spirit is. He is tenderhearted and so very kind, and He will move us to compassion when we allow Him to, as He knows the hope of the requested prayer. That way I will have His power and energy to help me. However, I still want to have compassion in my prayers—I *want* to feel it, so I will spend more time and give more thought regarding others' prayer requests. If I need to stir my compassion because I am a human and am subject to a lack of imagination sometimes when details are lacking, I will still think about something that will allow compassion to flow in through an open door however it can and that will, once the stirring begins, transfer it to the needs of my friends. I cannot allow my dignity and pride to keep me from looking under every rock for whatever tool can be found in order to become a more effective Christian.

I realized that whether we admit it or not, our prayers for other people's needs are not very fervent most of the time. We have become so calloused by life, crime, the speed with which life seems to be flying, TV, our jobs, and so many other things. It's hurry up, hurry up, hurry up; do this, do that; come here, go there. We barely have time or thought for real compassion. Feeling others' pain is not comfortable, so we condition ourselves to not be vulnerable. However, we need to feel the pain. Keeping up with our families and Satan's list of challenges drains a lot of our ability to love the way we should, and we are not practicing our faith on behalf of our Christian family in the right way, either. Neither are we resisting the devil enough, as James 4:7 tells us to do. If we were using more faith, along with more resistance against the devil, then we wouldn't be distracted at every turn and would be more submitted to God. Because we are born with a sinful nature, we do seem to have a tendency to focus more on the problem than on the answer. God's Word holds every answer.

Have you ever thought that prayer is really an effort from us to pull the power of God down onto a situation? That sounds so remarkable, to think that it could even be possible. Remember the power and greatness of God and who He is. Surely it requires more involvement and respect from us than an unfelt, unconcerned, almost egotistical approach. If we mean business with our prayers, we need to put our heart and loving concern into them, using the Word of God to help us pray and saying "It is written" as often as we can. These are taken from a few scriptures that are usually the first ones I say, such as: "It is written" (Is. 54:17) "No weapon formed against us shall prosper". (Is. 55:11) "The Word does not go forth void but accomplishes that which it is sent forth to do". (Rom. 8:31) "If God be for us who can be against us". (Is. 59:19) "When the enemy comes in, like a flood the spirit of the Lord will lift up a standard against him". (1 Pet. 2:24) "By His stripes we are healed". (Jas. 4:7) "Resist the devil and he will flee from you". A promise book is inexpensive and available at any Christian bookstore. It's a great little book to keep on hand, and promises are sorted by subject. That makes it much easier to be more exact in applying the word that fits a particular type situation. These promises are from God and are the Holy Scriptures. Trust them.

First Thessalonians 2:13 says that when we received the Word of God, we welcomed it not as words of men, but as truth that effectively works in us who believe. That word, effectively, implies a lot of energy. It would be much more beneficial to our families and friends, and more acceptable to God, if we would pray earnestly and effectively, with passion and zeal. As believers, we do pray. God ascribes righteousness to us because of Christ within us, so we know He hears our prayers. I am amazed and wonder about the power of Elijah's prayer. How many of us have stopped the rain for three years and six months, like Elijah? He was a man with a nature like ours, and he prayed earnestly (seriously, intensely, and deeply convinced), and the rain stopped. Later he prayed again, and Heaven gave back the rain and produced fruit. Do you know anybody who prays like that? We should be doing so ourselves—God says we can—or we should know at least one person who does, don't you think? If Elijah was a man with a nature like ours, and if we remember that "the heartfelt prayer of a righteous man availeth much" (James 5:16, NKJV), then if Elijah can have that kind of faith, we can too, if we believe and pray deeply convinced, as he did. We must of course make sure we're on the right path if we want to pray for something that will affect that many people so seriously! We always need to allow for our requests being considered by God, especially if other people are to be affected.

If your compassion needs to be stirred, as I am sure mine will again and again, let's draw it from the suffering of Jesus—the nails in His hands, the crown of thorns, His beard being pulled out of His face, the hell He had to descend into, and the weight of the sins of the world being placed on His shoulders. Be stirred, feel compassion, pray with sincerity, and feel it in your soul, then you can actually achieve results because God allows us to all the time, when we are sincere.

Can you imagine the power of an entire church praising with their hearts and souls, and praying earnest, effective, energized prayers? What's so hard about that, anyway? Why can't we do that? Come on, brave hearts, we can do it! Don't let people inhibit your efforts as a prayer warrior or as one giving praise to our

King of glory. Hold fast to the faith. This moving mountains isn't as simple as it sounds. Can we reach for the diligence and the depth of our commitment to Him and to each other, so that we really achieve amazing, Godly results? We often appear to just be scratching the surface of what is available through the power of God. He is waiting for us to take Him very seriously, to call on Him, seek Him, praise Him, walk in victory because of Him—and invite Him to appear as He did in Isaiah. He created the world with His awesome power.

> **Let's not settle for little, when great and mighty acts are available. Who do we think the recipients have been of great and mighty acts up till now? People like us. He offers His great promises, and it isn't His fault if we stop short. So let's not put up a stop sign to God, for goodness sake. Let's open the throttle. Why do we think that if we've reached a certain degree of success, it is acceptable to stop pressing our faith and pressing toward the prize?**

We can't use it all up—we can give it up, but using our faith just makes it stronger, bigger, and more successful.

Lord God almighty, fill this temple with Your glory!

Let me encourage you with these uplifting words of praise written by God, just for you. They are from the *Amplified Bible*.

> O Sing to the Lord a new song, for He has done marvelous things; His right hand and His holy arm have wrought salvation for Him. Make a joyful noise to the Lord, all the earth; break forth and sing for joy, yes, sing praises! Sing praises to the Lord with the lyre; with the lyre and the voice of melody. With the trumpets and sound of the horn make a joyful noise before the King, the Lord! Let the sea roar and all that fills it, the world

and those who dwell in it! Let the rivers clap their hands; together let the hills sing for joy before the Lord; for He is coming to judge [and rule] the world, and the peoples with equity. (Ps. 98 1-9)

Know—perceive, recognize and understand with approval—that the Lord is God. It is He Who has made us, not we ourselves [and we are His]! We are His people and the sheep of His pasture. Enter His gates with thanksgiving and with a thank offering, and into His courts with praise! Be thankful, and say so to Him, bless and affectionately praise His name! For the Lord is good; His mercy and loving-kindness are everlasting; His faithfulness and truth endure to all generations. (Ps.100:3–5)

Praise Him and *purposefully* bring glory to His holy name.

Anybody can be a child of God, but you have to want to be a servant. Clean out the clutter from your mind; fill your thoughts with your purpose in this life to love and to serve. Get back on track from when you first accepted Jesus. Become born again if you need to, and follow through. Remember who He is. Our reward is in Heaven and anything we can do to help usher in His Kingdom will be of good service. Just think of the day that you will be allowed to enter into the great throne room of God.

God bless you and I love you,
Dian

Chapter Eleven

The Power and the Glory

Our pastor had asked me to read a chapter from this book while it was still in progress, during a Sunday evening service. Because the children and teens were present in the sanctuary on Sunday evening, I had chosen the story about the fish in the middle of the road, as told in chapter 10. For two or three days before the service, the Shekinah glory had been in my heart and mind, and I was seeking His glory, a high-reaching goal. Shekinah is defined in *Merriam-Webster's Dictionary* as "the manifestation of the presence of God" or divine presence. Isaiah 6:1–4 describes an experiencing of that great and powerful manifestation. My worthiness from a human point of view is not required, because that would be dependent on the righteousness of man. My worthiness to Jesus was proven when He gave His life for me and you. My heart yearns after more and more of the revelation of God.

I thought about how I could pray a prayer requesting the manifestation of His glory, especially knowing that a spirit of timidity (not yet dealt properly with) could make such a prayer less effective in a public place. Then it came to me to simply place my fingers on the keyboard, close my eyes, and write the prayer that came into my heart. I do not know from where this prayer came, my spirit or my mind, but I do not believe that my mind did this on its own—especially after reading the results. Once again, a humble, willing heart sought the extraordinary and received extraordinary results. The following is the prayer that God put in my heart.

A Prayer for the Shekinah Glory

Father, we come before You with praise and thanksgiving in our hearts. We ask You to forgive us, Lord, for our sins and forgive us when we fail You. We declare, Father God, that we will forgive others, as You so willingly forgive us.

We are meek and humble, Lord, but our prayer is that we be strong in Your behalf, able to obtain a greater walk with You, and that we may be able to see more of Your presence. We know it's available, and whatever it takes, Lord, let us be willing to do it. There is no greater reward than having You as our Lord. Father, it is written that what You do for one You will do for all, and that You are no respecter of persons. Father, we are Your people and the sheep of Your pasture. You are grand, and we praise You. We know that we are members of the army of the Lord, and we are members of the body of Christ. Father, we are not lazy or tired—we are requesting a bigger assignment, we want more responsibility toward Your great cause.

Lord, we do not want to be in, or to stay put in, a comfort zone. Things run smoothly and routines are down pat, but Lord, we want some spiritual moving and shaking. It is our desire to strive for, seek for, long for, and do more for Your glorious presence. We need to do away with the status quo and get into the area of the supernatural with You. We know that, with Your help, we can maintain order, Lord, and still be able to be lifted up and out and to new heights. Lord, we want a new song—to see the hills sing for You, and the river clap its hands.

There is so much more beyond the surface, Father, and we are looking for the deep things of God. Help us break the mold.

Help us open the door. We are aware of miracles and of even greater things that are available to us, Father, and we need to see Your power loosed for us so that our eyes can see. We need our faith fired up so that achieving within the supernatural realm is as easy as believing it, as we should now be doing. Feeling Your presence in a supernatural way, whether it be in the magnificent Shekinah glory or any other form of Your design, would be a tremendous lift to get us up and out the door with Your mighty mission in mind.

Lord, we need insight and revelation. We need motivation and inspiration and drive. Lord, so that souls may be saved and blessings are given by Your hand through ours, please give us a vision of service toward the lost within our own communities, beyond what is normal in a modern-day American church. We want to be like the early church, Lord: filled with enthusiasm, to the point of being willing to die if need be, for the Gospel. We need stirring and sifting, Lord. My personal prayer is that I may be a member of the front lines in God's army, not someone back at the campfire. Help us, Lord.

Because we are children of Abraham and heirs according to the promise, Lord, we are pleading to see the manifestation of Your glory. We understand that this is a form of Your revealing Yourself to man where man does not die upon seeing. Whatever we need to do, whether it be in faith, charity, prayer, witnessing, or anything You show us or speak to us to do, it is our heart's desire to be in the presence of this magnificent revealing of Yourself, not for pride or wrong reasons, Lord, but for the pure, spiritual blessing and also the outreach and motivation it would bring to our area, far and wide. Lord, we need to be reminded that we are but flesh and have been born with a sinful nature. We need to be exposed to a force so pure and holy that we remember how unclean, undone, and corrupt we were before Jesus saved us, and how lost and miserable the world is around us.

Remembering would set us firmly into evangelism, with a determined heart, but our heart's desire to see Your glory is also because there could be no greater thing to see and be a part of, while in this body. We would not be vain, Lord, only exceedingly thankful and grateful. I know that You know my heart. I do not know how many requests You receive per day for the manifestation of the Shekinah glory to be seen in a church, Lord, but I earnestly pray that this is the one You will answer today.

We understand that we cannot earn this holy blessing and are very respectful in our request, Father—not in any way wanting to ask amiss, but I personally want You to know that if that event should occur, my life would be overtaken and seem complete, in the sense that my eyes along with my spirit could testify about having been in Your presence while totally humbled and completely amazed. I would be able to carry the message of whatever words that You would give me about having seen, but not having been harmed by, the fire and the glory of the living God. For all who stand with me in this, as a sincere prayer, please say, "So let it be." Say yes, Amen.

The Testimony

The following is a true testimony of what happened shortly after I spoke this prayer for the Shekinah glory during a Sunday night service at House of Mercy Church in Morris Chapel, Tennessee. I understand that this may sound strange, and it is most certainly not an average church service. But stop and think: for God to show up supernaturally to a group of His children who were practically begging Him to doesn't seem so odd. We just aren't accustomed to expecting that kind of manifestation from Him—but why not? Complacency and lack of knowledge are keeping Him away. If He did show up in this manner in your church, don't you think that people's knees might give way? Please hear the message of my soul. God is mighty, He is real, and He is able. We just don't seek Him in a powerful, extraordinary way. My, my, what we are missing. Human words are inadequate to describe the impact and dynamics of it.

The prayer was followed by two inspired songs that were so fitting for that particular service, only God, (knowing in advance of course) could have chosen the titles and the spiritually submitted Christians who performed them. The atmosphere became absolutely intense with the presence of God over the entire congregation. Nearly everybody fled to the altar. People fell from the presence of God's spirit, praying, crying, and being overwhelmed in the most powerful, amazing way. I had returned to my seat following the prayer to be blessed by the rest of the service when God took over completely. I wanted to maintain the most bowed-down, praying, and praising position of my life. The floor wasn't low enough—not because I felt unworthiness but because of the tremendous, weighty honor and respect that came from being in His presence … Never in my life have I ever felt such a presence. My sister in Christ, who was also my Sunday school teacher, said there was actually a mist over the platform. That presence was felt all over the room. It was a holy presence, and pressure—not of a negative force, but rather requiring complete respect and surrender; not in a demanding way, but in a way of being saturated with love and reverence, being unable to make normal use of your natural strength—just seized and yielded to an adoring, magnificent spiritual being—our mighty God, our holy Lord.

That experience elevated my spirit to new and wonderful heights and gave me far more and greater future expectations—not from God, but from myself, having witnessed such a revelation of power. Tears were streaming down my face; awestruck wonder and joy overwhelmed me beyond my strength, yet I was unhurt and unharmed, while I kept slipping nearly underneath the pew in front of me, then pulling back up just to slip down again. I did not want it to end; nobody did. The pastor has said that at least one miracle had occurred, with a young boy being delivered from I know not what, but thank God for it, anyway. There is no telling how many other great results came out of that encounter. Some may still be in progress, as the result of God coming among us that night. How holy, how awesome and real.

The pastor had fallen from the power of the spirit; folks were laying all over the place, on the altar, the floor, and the benches (just as when John the Revelator beheld the risen Christ, he fell at His feet as if dead in Rev. 1:17, Amp; just as Balaam's donkey laid down under him, and Balaam fell on his face on the ground before the Angel of the Lord—Num. 22:28, Amp). It was so honest and inspiring toward renewing and motivating the human heart. Nothing of an earthly nature could compare. Seek until you find it. The renewal you will walk in, and the reality from such an encounter with the power and pure love of God, will forever set you on course to achieve your true mission for Him in life. Seek a personal encounter on a higher plane, for it is real and can actually occur. Nothing in our normal world can ever compare.

When I left the parking lot that night, I knew that I had been in a higher realm. The necessity of having to drive the car and do normal things after such an experience was difficult. No one left the church right away; we had witnessed God's presence and had felt His supernatural power. I telephoned family members, trying to tell them about the most awesome service that I had ever witnessed. It was life changing—and how I would love to witness it again! Nothing has ever come close to matching the extreme amazement of that evening, when the power of the Holy Spirit showed up either as, or similar to, the great and mighty Shekinah glory of the living, one and only, real God. Thank You, Father, from the bottom of my heart—what a wonder, what a surprise, what a gift from You. Thank You still again, Father God. My heart is filled with love for You. You are so mighty and worthy to be praised. Thank You, Lord, thank You.

Love,
Dian

Chapter Twelve

What Does Being a Christian Mean to Me?

This question was first asked in chapter 4: What does being a Christian mean to me? Because Christ is the first and the last, the alpha and the omega, the ever living one, and the beginning and the end, my heart's desire is to present my personal continuation of more and more of God till it fills the soul. Hebrews 5:11–14 (Amp) explains how, when learning the first principles of God, we are on milk instead of solid food, but sooner or later we need to become more skilled in the doctrine of righteousness, and solid food is for Christians who train their senses and mental faculties through practice to distinguish between good and evil, and between what is noble and what is contrary to the divine law. Unfortunately, some have yet to make it even to the milk.

Being a Christian also includes understanding our relationship with our spiritual home land of Israel. Jesus, when born as a human man, was in the lineage of King David. When we accept Jesus as our Savior, we become grafted into the Tribe of Judah that He was born into, making our lineage the same as His as a man. In the supernatural realm Jesus is King and is the Son of God, giving us the honor of being His children. So in all respects we have a tremendous heritage. The word "Hebrews" as titled in the Bible refers to "a group of Messianic Jews." The Book of Hebrews in our Bible is powerful, but the nation of Israel is Jewish, not Christian. During Jesus's walk on the earth, God constantly appealed to the Jewish people to believe that He had sent Jesus Christ, as the Messiah, for their salvation. If you read the first four chapters of Hebrews, you can easily see how God compared the people then being presented with the Gospel to the ones who spent forty years in the wilderness due to their disobedience and unbelief. We don't just have America, or our own countries to pray for and reach out to with the Gospel. This is an appeal for your prayers for the nation of Israel and the Jewish people. Why? Because God still wants them to believe in Jesus as Messiah and laid out some divine directions for us to live by, and our standing by Israel is one of them. It is His chosen nation. If God loves Israel and has given them the honor of His protection and love, then we as His children are obliged to. It is very important to Him. Therefore, being a Christian means loving and praying for Israel as God wants us to.

It is also very important not to have a casual attitude toward the Old Testament. Study will reveal more of the enormity of God's intelligence and power that are evident in the ways in which He tells us an obvious truth, while weaving in a concealed prophetic truth, which a casual reader would not realize. He does that effortlessly, throughout the entire Bible—with line upon line and precept upon precept. Wouldn't it be wonderful to see some of the parallel ties detailed in hidden intricacies between the Old Testament and the New Testament, which are not revealed in casual reading? You will encounter *total intelligence* in Person. It will be fascinating, and your respect and awe toward the Bible being both Divine and Holy cannot help but increase. You will see part of the picture of God choosing Israel in Deuteronomy chapter four. Using the *Amplified Bible* will help for clarity. In the first verse, He says for Israel to listen and He will teach them. In other words, He will give them His instructions for them (and us) to follow. In verse 31 He tells them that He does not forget the covenant He made with their fathers before they were born. The children of Israel become examples of His power, love, His infallible word revealed in the keeping of covenants, and His desire for mankind. In verses 39-40, He tells them (and us too, through Jesus) how to help our lives go well. The covenant He made with Abraham, which we are privileged to claim, is described in Deuteronomy chapter twenty-eight.

Our Christian heritage was born from Hebraic roots, as was the man, Jesus. The thief on the cross was the first man whose sins were covered by the shed blood of our Jewish-born Jesus in Jerusalem. God has used Israel from the beginning. He said in Deuteronomy 7:7 (Amp), that they were the "fewest of all people." In the next verse He says *again* that He is keeping the oath which He swore to their fathers. Don't we want to recognize and choose to be under these covenants that God intends to keep for the inheritors of His Kingdom? We must not regard lightly this powerful privilege that we have been given to align ourselves with Israel and to honor and pray for her and her people—both naturally and spiritually. Remember that we are spiritually grafted in to the Tribe of Judah through the lineage of Jesus. Be a blessing to His Kingdom and help those who are not yet His born-again ones be restored to their right standing with Him, so that we are cooperating with God and not putting ourselves into a state of ill will. Heaven forbid. (And it does.)

When I first heard Hebraic teaching regarding temple worship I must admit that I ignorantly wondered what that had to do with me during this day and time. I thought that I was there to hear a sermon that I could take to heart and apply to my spiritual growth, and not be hearing about "history." I have now repented with all my heart for that misunderstanding. When you hear a good preacher/teacher who puts it all into words that you understand, you will be amazed by the depth and wonder it will bring to your soul. Hebraic research into the complex, intricate weaving of God's plan throughout the Old Testament firmly *predicts* and *presents* Jesus, the end-times, the gathering-in (our English word used for that is "Rapture"), tribulation, and many exciting biblical events. It is like someone pouring gold dust into your cupped hands. The closest that I could get to being a student in a class that explains the relationship between scriptures from the New Testament being rooted and grounded in the Old Testament was to order my first six DVDs from Pastor Perry Stone. His ministry program, called "Manna-Fest" is seen on Daystar, TBN, and Inspiration Ministry (INSP). He has a tremendous love and vast knowledge of how (quote) "Jesus is *concealed* in the Old Testament and *revealed* in the New Testament." The amazing information is that, for instance, the Old Testament worship, items of temple furniture, the requirements for the way a priest's garments were made, the law of the first fruits, and reasons for different feasts clearly are reflected in why Jesus said and did most everything that He did say and do. The Old Testament was written in the Hebrew language and the importance of those practices that God taught the Hebrew people were so important to God that they have continued to be represented or referred to in many ways through Jesus's ministry in the New Testament. Understanding that, and that God had written it, concealed except to a serious searcher, as underlying, interesting information in the Old Testament well before the New Testament was written, is so extraordinary.

This is a fact that many don't want to face. The Jewish people do not struggle with the language of the Old Testament. They would if it had been written in English. It had to be translated from their language to ours for us to understand it.

There are parallels woven throughout, both clear and concealed, together presenting a whole new world of validity, verification, explanation, and confirmation which you discover when you watch the plan of God unfold with additional references to many of the reasons and practices explained through Hebraic teaching. A cord of three strands cannot be broken. For illustration purposes, let's say there are three strands. There is one representing the Old Testament, one the New Testament, and Jesus. God begins braiding the strands together with "In the beginning" (Gen. 1:1) overlapping, weaving one cord, covering another, entwining all with His last words, "Yes, come Lord Jesus" (Rev. 22:20) just before the final blessing.

Thank you, Thank you God, for the preachers, teachers, and ministries that present our firmly based, bound and established spiritual roots, born in ancient times through Abraham, the Jewish prophets, priests, customs, laws, worship, and people. These are the foundation of our Christian Gospel. Please don't skip over the importance of Israel and the Jewish people having produced our Christian heritage through ancient times, and whom are continuing in these modern, troubled times to be absolutely vital to us right to the very end. We have a responsibility toward them, in God's eyes, but it is not burdensome. It is our destiny. God, Jesus, and the Holy Spirit are presented in the Old and New Testament.

I am reminded, for use as an example, of the scripture in First Corinthians 13:12 in the *Amplified Bible* that says, "For now we are looking in a mirror that gives only a dim (blurred) reflection [of reality as in a riddle or enigma], but then [when perfection comes] we shall see in reality and face to face! Now I know in part (imperfectly); but then I shall know and understand fully and clearly, even in the same manner as I have been fully and clearly known and understood [by God]." I imagine Jesus standing between two mirrors which represent the Old and New Testaments. When we look at Him in the dim, blurred reflection that is how we see Him in the Old Testament. But when we look at Him in the other (New Testament) mirror, He is much clearer. Thank God for the day that will come when we see Him neither dimly, blurred, nor in a mirror at all, but face to face! In the meantime, men like Perry Stone and David Cerullo are providing us with a uniquely wonderful, much clearer picture of our very real, supremely intelligent, tremendously active, mysteriously brilliant God.

Our complacency and self-centeredness have caused many of us to ignore the directive from God to pray for Israel. Psalm 122:6 (KJV) says, "Pray for the peace of Jerusalem: they shall prosper that love thee." God did first send Jesus to the Jews, and there are many Messianic Jews (i.e., Jews who believe in Jesus Christ as their Messiah). Israel is called the Holy Land. Neither the United States nor any other country is called that. It would be to our great advantage to be supportive of the country where Christianity began, and where Jesus was born. Israel needs our love, support, and prayers; she is our spiritual homeland on earth. During the last few weeks, my heart has been so touched by a mental picture that continues to come to mind. Each time my heart has felt moved in tenderness, often to tears. I certainly made no effort to improve on the picture, because each time it came to mind, I thought that it was complete. The final version presents a scene that I now believe refers to all to whom the Gospel has not yet been received—both the Jews and the Gentiles.

The scripture in Deuteronomy 4:11–12 inspired my thoughts. Picture a great mountain ablaze with fire. Out of the midst of the fire, dark, heavy clouds, and rolling smoke billow up, filling the sky. From out of that comes the great voice of God, which could be heard and distinguished in spite of the roaring flames (what a mighty God we serve—what enormous power). A crowd of people huddled tightly together some distance across the hot desert sand. They knew that they had heard the voice of God. All that was visible of Him to me were His eyes, to the upper left of the mountain. Those eyes come to my mind often now; they were very intense, somewhat annoyed, but kind. Then from the base of the mountain, visible for all to see, Jesus, Prince of Peace, came striding forth. He was dressed in a long white robe, tied at the waist, and He very intently moved toward the people, bridging the gap between the magnificent God of the fire of the mountain and the people who had separated from Him because of doubt and fear. From the back of the crowd of people, a small figure struggled to cross the sand trying to get to Jesus—but stumbled, fell, appeared to be crippled. As the figure approached Jesus, I realized that it was me. Being small and insignificant, I reached Jesus as He continued toward the people. He stopped, looked at me, reached out His precious hand, and asked, "Why have you come from behind the crowd to me?"

"Because in you there is living water, cleanness, healing, and light," I said.

"My journey is near the end," said He, "and still my people are not saved."

Said I, "As Isaiah was sent, Lord—even as tiny an impression as I—please, please also use and send me."

My tears are shed over the hope for people to see and recognize the huge importance placed by God on the nation of Israel, their well-being, and the salvation of the lost.

The dispensation of the Gospel, which took in the Gentiles and rejected the Jews (because of their unbelief), did not change God's word of promise to Abraham, who did believe.

> **Romans 9:4-5 (Amp) states, "For they are Israelites, and to them belongs God's adoption [as a nation] and the glorious (Shekinah) Presence. With them were the special covenants made, to them was the Law given. To them [the temple] worship was revealed and [God's own] promises announced. To them belongs the patriarchs, and as far as His natural descent was concerned from them is the Christ, Who is exalted and supreme over all— God, blessed forever!" Amen—so let it be.**

Most people give very little thought to the importance placed by God on Israel. If it is important enough for Him to actually give us directives and scriptures regarding our behavior toward Israel, then we should take Israel very seriously, because God means business. We once had a bumper sticker in our store that said, "When God speaks, even E. F. Hutton listens." The sticker referred to a TV ad that had glorified E. F. Hutton as the final authority on investment advice. God's authority is the highest forever and always, and we should honor His instructions in all areas. Do it to please Him, whether you understand it or not. God is not pleased with our behavior and neglect concerning the complacency and self-centeredness that many of us show in general, and specifically by ignoring His regard for Israel.

Also, we are to fulfill God's directives by showing ourselves strong on His behalf, lifting up and helping those He directs us to. Help gather in those who are lost, including the Jewish people, make all clean by the Word, and prepare to present His body of believers when He comes for His church. I specify Israel because of God's concern for her. I specify America in this country because she is our natural homeland. The entire world needs to know the Gospel, but did you know that I have met people from other countries who have come to America as missionaries of the Gospel message? Does that not shock you? It certainly did me, but now that I have gotten used to the idea, we need more of them.

My sincere prayer is for every reader to consider the concept of turning your attention away from the world and turn your eyes toward Jesus. If you have never become born again, then you have forfeited your soul to be destined for hell. This is the Gospel in its simplest form: Heaven or hell. By not choosing Heaven, you automatically choose the other. You are the only one who can change your destination.

So I ask again, "What does being a Christian mean to me?" The continuation of the answer from where I left off in chapter 4 is what I offer to you as a song for your heart, and as a very genuine encouragement for you to pursue Jesus the Messiah, born in Bethlehem, our Savior, the Son of God.

My love for God is real. My faith, hope, and trust for Him are real. All of my testimonies are true, plus many more not yet told. The extraordinary thing about this life that has been so good, and that continues to be filled with the wonder of God, is that who I have been in life, plus some of my poor choices, have at times made me seem a very unlikely candidate for such favor. And that is the point. All He needs is a willing, believing, and repentant heart. His favor is available to any and all who come to Him in sincerity. It truly is a very special, wonderful existence to live by faith and as a child of God. Be my sister or brother in the Lord, delight in the blessed good life, and let your little light shine as a member of the family of God.

These are my words spoken by the help of His spirit.

The almighty God, Creator and ruler of Heaven, gave us the way, the truth, and the life. He wanted us to be in fellowship with Him, and hallelujah to God for lifting me into a place above the ways of the world, with joyful anticipation of life instead of dread.

There are no words to express the miracle and wonder that comes through the love of God to us. It resulted in the shedding of His blood through His son Jesus, who died for the remitting of our sins because we had no acceptable sacrifice to give. God gave Jesus for us. He also gave us the immeasurable right to one day see Him face-to-face, and to now live in union and fellowship with Him as a friend and a Father to us. He gives us the right to have victory over the pains and problems of life, and He tells us how to resist Satan and his demons. He gives us the right to call on His name in faith, believing and watching in awe as our almighty God performs miracles of deliverance, healing, restoring, encouragement, and joy-filled wonders. He gives us the precious, gentle Holy Spirit to comfort and guide us. He gives us the privilege and joy of sharing His always true and always dependable word of hope and promise with others, so that they too can know and share in the greatest life on earth.

He opens His storehouse of Heaven and pours blessings on our heads. He gives us the great confidence of knowing that no matter what happens to us or what anyone does or threatens, no person can keep us from God or Heaven. He totally diminishes the problems of the entire planet with as little as one word spoken by Him.

He gives us purpose, direction, meaning, will, and strength to keep reaching for more of the Kingdom life. I live to fulfill my heart's desire to have, know, and be more like Jesus. I am eager to be challenged, to be able to express it, to tell it, to yell it if need be, and to live it. It has thus far made my life count for something and has given me gladness to live by and a great job, reaping rewards of blessings and the greatest, most exciting prize at the end of good days on earth.

How can anybody not want this? We need to tell it. My life, my blessings, my health—whatever good that I have is because of my Jesus, and it's all available to all of us. By whatever grace that caused me to receive and pursue the purity, love, and light of our God, I will be eternally grateful. It is my life, my joy, my love. Some other words that express my attitude toward God are awesome, glorious, holy, magnificent, and powerful. God is my Savior, the shepherd of my heart, the one in whom I confidently trust.

I love my Lord, and I love my brothers and sisters in Him. God bless you and keep you. Be glad when they say unto you, "Let us go to the house of the Lord." Be first at the door, sit near the front, and pray that if the anointing flows, you'll be under it too. Go to the altar when the preacher calls folks to come and receive whatever blessings that he says. You need it all in order to stay strong and ready, and if you aren't having that particular need at that time, go for someone else who is, or substitute your own need instead. Don't pass these opportunities by. Get it, love it, live it. Take all you can get, and then go forth and conquer in Jesus's name—and *share it*. It's the mightiness and truth of the holy Gospel.

God bless, and I love you.
Love,
Dian

Rejoice in the Risen Savior

The Christmastime infant has grown up,
You know, and now
He's not a child.

Oh, the risen Jesus—all power and light,
No longer a baby, meek and mild.
He's ruling the earth with force and might
As our strong Savior—not a child.

I look toward the glory of His shining face
And think of the honor that He deserves.
Then around me in this worldly place,
I see the dishonor that He's being served.

Give praise to the glory of His present reign.
He judges and governs and gives us salvation!
To the ruling Jesus, not a newborn king—
Let this glad tiding be our exaltation.

His glorious presence Revelation describes:
Flashing eyes like flames of fire,
Hair showy white, face noon-day bright,
With a two-edged sword and all God's power.

The first and the last, with it all in His hands.
It's true angels bow and demons do tremble.
He's making His stand for the souls of man.
This is the Christ we should remember.

He wants your praise—He's saved your soul.
He's returning soon, so stand up and sing!
Forget the flurry and tinsel of gold.
Behold, God's son, your Savior—your King!
Jesus loves you and so do I. God bless you,

Dian

209

References

Amplified Bible (Amp). Grand Rapids: Zondervan, 1965.

The Bible, King James Version (KJV).

Dake, Finis Jennings. *God's Plan for Man.* Lawrenceville: Dake, 1977.

Dake's Annotated Reference Bible, King James Version. Lawrenceville: Dake, 1963.

Hayford's Bible Handbook. Ed. Jack W. Hayford. Nashville: Thomas Nelson, 1995.

Henry, Matthew. *Matthew Henry's Commentary on the Whole Bible.* Ed. Rev. Leslie F. Church. Grand Rapids: Zondervan, 1961.

The Matthew Henry Study Bible, King James Version. Ed. A. Kenneth Abraham. Grand Rapids: Word, 1994, 1997.

Merriam-Webster's New Collegiate Dictionary. 1975 ed.

The Spirit Filled Life Bible, New King James Version (NKJV). Ed. Jack W. Hayford. Nashville: Thomas Nelson, 1991.

Stern, David H. *Jewish New Testament.* Clarksville: Messianic Jewish Publishers, 1989.

Stern, David H. *Jewish New Testament Commentary.* Clarksville: Messianic Jewish Publishers, 1992.

Strong, James. *Strong's Exhaustive Concordance of the Bible.* Nashville: Abingdon, 1980.

Thompson, Frank Charles. *The Thompson Exhaustive Topical Bible, King James Version.* Ed. Paul Hillman, John Jauchen. Indianapolis: B. B. Kirkbride Bible Co., 1997.

Wuest, Kenneth S. *The New Testament: An Expanded Translation.* Iowa Falls: Riverside, 1961.

CPSIA information can be obtained at www.ICGtesting.com
Printed in the USA
LVOW11s1802050814

397657LV00001B/136/P